TURN AROUND YOUR BUSINESS BY 5PM

HOW TO WIN IN A LOSING ECONOMY

MAURICE STEIN

Content

Introduction

Over the last few years, the world economy has gone through some major changes. Every industry and business has been affected by it, and some of the largest corporations – who, for decades, were the symbol of success – have closed their doors for good, leaving the general public shocked and confused.

At the same time, though, the Internet and all of technology have advanced at lightning speed, creating new industries and opening up new opportunities that never existed before. We are now seeing radical changes in the market place and feel that there are many new ways of incorporating them to benefit our business, but we find it difficult to decide where to get started and what steps to take towards change.

Over the last 12 years, I've had the opportunity to coach business owners in how to develop and grow their businesses. With gentle guidance, I helped them make the necessary adjustments to accommodate new and changing economic situations. Simply and plainly, my goal with this book is to share what I have learned over these many years and so to help you take your business to the next level.

As running a business requires combinations of skill, talent and the right set of beliefs, reading this book will expand your thinking and arm it with new, empowering beliefs that make you a better decision maker. Additionally, this will give you a fresh look at some of the aspects of your company's fundamental components.

Some of the concepts in this book may seem very simple and basic. Are you really implementing them into your business, though? If not, ask yourself what it is that's stopping you from doing so. The knowledge of things will not make you successful; their utilization will.

This book would never be possible without the wonderful entrepreneurs I have had the pleasure of dealing with. They gave me the opportunity to work with them and their teams. They brought me in to face their challenges together, and then let me create positive solutions. As we applied and constantly tweaked those newfound solutions, we ultimately found the correct approach. For all their trust and belief in me – I would like to thank them. For their friendship and united growth – I cherish them. It is their credit that I got to where I am today.

My special thanks to Mayer Silver (www.mayersilver.com) for editing this book and to Joseph Blumenfeld (www.gcny-marketing.com) for his constant support with design and strategic direction.

As you turn the page, we will start out on a joint effort, a journey through the world of business and commerce. We will take a trip together and find the finer points that will, God willing, help anchor your business for a profitable future.

To your success!
Maurice

Chapter 1

WHERE ARE YOU NOW?

What Is Happening to Your Business?

Is there something wrong with your business, but you are not quite sure what it is? Do you feel that you know your industry well enough and still can't put your finger on what exactly has changed?

Have you experienced any of the following?

- Decreased sales
- Customer attrition – clients who have gone out of business or are struggling to pay their bills
- Money loss due to ineffective advertising
- A feeling that time has dramatically slowed down or sped up
- A loss of the excitement you had when you started the business

Yes, the economy is bad; we may even be somewhere between coming out of one recession and sliding into another. Many businesses, however, are doing very well, growing and thriving. Some of these may even be in your industry – even be your competitors. Some may have benefitted from ideas you consider your own.

If you feel that your business is failing and that it's too late to save it, then bear this in mind: You've built your business up once and you can do it again. The economy has changed a lot since you started out. Maybe you

"In times of rapid change, experience could be your worst enemy."

J. Paul Getty

didn't adopt the changes necessary to stay ahead in the game, but it is never too late. You can find your way back to success and turn your business around quickly. Let's begin with where you are now.

Get Clear on Where You Are

If you want to turn your business around by 5 pm today, the first thing to know is which way you're facing now! Get the facts in clear writing. You may think, "Come on! Can't we just talk about the solutions? I know my problems in my sleep, why do I have to write them down?"

While I agree that you may know your problems, you still have to write them down. And here's why: When we are faced with a situation [in life or in business] that we don't like, there are always two parts to it:

1) The true facts of the problem or situation

2) The emotions that we attach to them

For example, if sales are down from previous years, there will be a factual, declined sales number. But when we think about that fact, many thoughts and emotions are

"Life is 10 % what happens to you and 90% how you respond to it."

Lou Holtz

generated. While these are **not** facts, we convince ourselves that they are in the same category.

Here is the challenge in fixing the problem: Instead of just dealing with the fact that sales are down and coming up with a list of solutions, we add a long list of emotions to fix as well. We see it all as a list of musts to correct, and doing so turns whole task into an impossible feat.

Sometimes, when a client tells me that their sales numbers are going down, it's very clear that this fact is but a small portion of their worries. For example, a client might say, "My sales are down for the last 18 months. Do you have any ideas what we can do about it?" Mentally, however, they finish their train of thought with, "I don't know what I am going to do about it... If this goes on for another few months (and I know it will), I will be broke and will lose the building I am in. I will have to let go of my employees and I might even lose my house... There is nothing I can do about it, because I have tried everything possible and I know this business as well as anyone else... I promised my... that I will talk to an expert so I called you... Now just tell me that I am right and there is nothing to do and let me get back to my worrying..."

Perhaps you don't think like that, but you probably know people who do, and it creates a bubble that is tough to get out of.

It Is Painful But Worth It!

Humans have an interesting habit of holding onto problems without getting down to the details. We may know that we have a problem in our business, but we don't seem to get down to the details of exactly what the problem is. This creates a false belief that we are not yet fully responsible to do something about the problem since we are still looking into it. We take this route because as soon as we know exactly what the problem is, we will have to take action and make changes – and we fear change, not knowing the results we will get.

This is the same reason why most people have tons of stuff piled up on their desks and throughout their office: it gives a false sense of being busy. In reality, a clean desk ushers in a clear mind, and we are more productive by focusing only on the one-two projects we are currently working on.

The simplicity, however, of knowing and doing exactly what we have to do right now feels scary, and so we would rather be surrounded by things and commotions for a (false) sense of security, even at the cost of productivity. It's not logical, but we don't live life based on logic. We live life based on our emotions and back these up with "just enough" logic in order to *feel* good about our illogical emotions.

Logic dictates that when you have a problem or are unhappy with the way your life or business is going, you sit down and be very clear and very specific about what is going on and what is or is not working and has to change.

When I listen to a new client complaining that his business is struggling, I will ask for some basic information in order to understand his situation. For example, I will ask for the amount of sales per month, the amount of sales per department or product category, the average markup on products or services, the overhead of the business, and so on and so forth.

It amazes me that most of the time the business owner doesn't even know his numbers, but assures me they are all available through the bookkeeper. The bookkeeper, in turn, often explains that she does not have all the numbers because her job is to keep records for tax purposes and not to measure productivity or the business' true net profit!

It would be irresponsible of me to give any business owner guidance without knowing those numbers; so would it be unwise for you to make any changes to your business without knowing the same. Sometimes it takes weeks until my client figures out the real numbers he needs. What always puzzles me is why this isn't first priority...

The Numbers Don't Lie

The first thing you want to do is get clear knowledge of all your numbers. If you can't, you need to implement a process that will give you those numbers going forward.

I am not an accountant, and, like most entrepreneurs, I don't love numbers. I do, however, know that we all need to look at the basic numbers in order to get a clear understanding of where our business stands.

There are a lot of numbers important in a business. Let's take a look at the top numbers that you want to have at your fingertips at all times.

SALES

GROSS SALES

The total number of gross sales that you got into your business for the last 24 hours, week, month or whatever time period makes sense in your business. The definition of "gross sales" is any money that your business received as a result of selling a product or service.

SALES BREAKDOWN

Most businesses have different categories of products or services. The more you can break your sales reports down into categories the easier it will be for you to see trends, and to spot any changes.

Categories would include any of the following:
- Different types of products or services.
- Different ways of distributing your product or service. For example wholesale vs. retail, online vs. offline, etc.
- Different locations of your business. Physical location of your stores, or your sales numbers based on region or state.
- Different price points – sizes – colors – packaging.

Such information helps a lot when it comes to making decisions on how to improve your business. It will show you where you have the biggest growth potential and which areas need the most focus.

EXPENSES

There are many types and groups, and you want to be clear on where each expense belongs.

C-O-G-S

'Costs of goods sold' (COGS) is what it costs you to purchase or manufacture your product or service. This might be a simple number if you are a wholesaler buying and selling a line of products, or it might be complicated to figure out, if you are manufacturing.

From experience I have seen that most people have this number wrong. They think they know what their costs are. They use their memory and logic to create numbers in their imagination based on what they remember them to be or based on what they think makes sense. Unless you actually look at the invoices you will never know.

Remember that you have to include all costs, including shipping costs to get the product to your location, commissions that you have to pay to brokers or sales people, etc.

In most cases, the cost of goods sold changes as the sales increase. The more sales we have, the less the cost of buying or manufacturing are, either because we have more buying power and we can negotiate a better price or because our existing overhead can handle a lot more than it currently does without increasing expenses.

The challenge is that we might think that we know our cost of goods sold based on the number of sales we did in the past or hope to do in the future. This is not the real number, though! If we want to be realistic with where are now, we have to look at the real cost of goods based on current sales.

FIXED EXPENSES

Fixed expenses include all business expenses that are ongoing, such as payroll, rent, utilities, trade shows, etc.

In most cases you have to look at a longer period of time in order to a clear picture. If you take a 12-month period and look at all of your expenses, it will give you a good snapshot of your fixed expenses. You also want to split the expenses by each department or category.

For example, if you have a few stores, you want to know your fixed expenses for each one. If you have a wholesale and retail department, you want to know your expenses for each. Sometimes you will have fixed expenses that are shared between the departments – e.g. if you have one bookkeeper for both – those expenses can be split between the departments.

NON-FIXED EXPENSES

Any and all bills that are occasional and not ongoing [such as moving into a new place or expenses of a marketing campaign to launch a new product line etc.] are considered 'non-fixed' expenses.

Some non-fixed expenses will only happen once and some of them will come up every two or three years. If you have a big one-time expense, like moving into a new place, you can look at it as a one-time thing and not include it in the overall profit-and-loss of the business. On the other hand, you DO have to include some non-fixed expense into your business planning, because some non-fixed expenses always occur.

NET PROFIT

You want to get the net profit for each department or category in your business by looking at the total sales and minus the COGS and other expenses.

THE BOTTOM LINE

Here is an example of an actual snapshot of a business:

Total sales in the last 12 months = $2,427,000

Total sales in the last 12 months in the wholesale department = $1,890,000

Total sales in the last 12 months in the retail department = $537,000

Total sales in the last 30 days = $230,000

Total sales in the last 30 days in the wholesale department = $146,000

Total sales in the last 30 days in the retail department = $84,000

Total of COGS in the last 12 months = $1,040,000

Total COGS in the last 12 months for the wholesale department = $780,800

Total COGS in the last 12 months for the retail department = $259,200

Total fixed overhead in the last 12 months = $669,600

Total fixed overhead in the last 12 months for the wholesale department = $462,200

Total fixed overhead in the last 12 months for the retail department = $207,400

Total non-fixed expenses in the last 12 months = $290,000

Total non-fixed expenses in the last months for the wholesale department = $176,900

Total non-fixed expenses in the last months for the retail department = $113,100

Total net profit in the last 12 months = $427,400

Total net profit in the wholesale department = $470,100

Total net profit in the retail department = $-42,700

When I first met this client he knew that things have changed, expenses have gone up, and sales on the retail side of the business has slowed down. But he didn't know his real numbers, and even if we had made changes we wouldn't know how to measure their effectiveness to know which changes really matter.

It took us about one month to get all the numbers organized. We then designed a plan together to reduce the overhead costs at the retail side of things and increase sales with new marketing projects.

Who is Your Customer?

Knowing your customer and why they are buying from you is one of the important parts of knowing your business. Frankly, the more you know your customers, the easier it will be to make the right adjustments to keep them with your company for the long run. It also helps in bringing in new customers.

When I ask clients, "Who are your customers?" I get a variety of answers like:

- Everyone is my customer...
- I know my customers. Don't worry about it...
- I know every one of my customers...
- We can run a report on my customer list if you like...

You might assume that you know your customers when you see orders coming in and people buying out, but that doesn't mean you know them or about them.

Even as you meet your customers at trade shows, bear in mind that you are only meeting that small percentage of customers who have chosen to attend. In addition to that, you are likely focused on what you want to sell them and not on why they want to buy from you at the event.

Knowing your customers means that you have a deep understanding of their needs, their lifestyles, their options, and their decision-making. You might be surprised to learn why people buy your products or services. The reason why they buy from you and not from your competitor might be completely different than what you think. Knowing the real reasons can make a major difference in the way you approach your business and how you run your sales and marketing.

JEWELRY FOR FISHING!

While working with a client who was selling jewelry online, we noticed that his client base was very diversified. While some people were buying a mixture of different items to resell in their stores, others were buying large quantities of one item. I asked the owner and staff if they could explain those buying patterns to me. Their answer was: "What's the difference? As long as they buy and pay, who cares?"

Since sales were going down, it was very important to me to understand why those customers were buying. We had to find a way of increasing sales by building stronger relationships with existing customers and finding new ones.

After a few hours on the phone with customers I learned that within his customer base there were two unique customer groups. One group included costume designers for stage performers who sewed together special jewelry stones on the gowns and headpieces. The other group *was full of wholesalers who sold to fishermen clubs and catalogues in the fishing industry. A little research taught us that some fishermen used specific, colored crystals on their hooks to lure the fish in.*

Learning about two new industries that had an interest in their product was a complete shock to everyone in the company. I put separate sales people to call suppliers in each of these markets, offering them special pricing on the products they had an interest in.

I also created an ad that went into the most popular fishing magazines. We placed another ad into a fashion magazine written specifically for stage performance designers. Within six months we had built a substantial amount of new clients and business in those two areas.

None of this would have happened if we didn't take the time to really know the customers and their reason of purchase!

When experts study the success of Apple and its founder Steve Jobs (1955-2011), they attribute much of the success of its products to Jobs' ability to understand the future needs of his customers even before they knew it themselves. Jobs would ask, "What would people enjoy having that does not exist yet?" He would then create the products that would fulfill those future needs. When he launched his products, customers would realize that "That's exactly what I need!" and they would wait in line for hours to buy them.

You might have a product or service that has a very broad customer base (like Apple does), or you might have a product for a very specific base only (diving equipment, for example). In either case, there are always specifics that you can learn about your customers and their needs or uses of your products. It will help you improve your product or service, gain new markets and keep your current client base happy.

Let's look at some of the basic things that you should know about your customers:

AGE

What is the age range that your product appeals to? Is it a narrow age range like kids between age 6-12, or does it have a broader age appeal like women between the ages of 18 and 45?

Knowing your customers' age is important and very relevant when you are deciding on price, marketing strategies, incentives, packaging design, distribution places, etc.

If your product has a specific client age, it might be worthwhile to research if there is any additional age group that might have a need for it. You may find that another age group would be interested in your product or service if you modify it a little according to their specific needs. Making these modifications can open up a new market for you where you would have little or no competition.

O ne of my friends with experience in Facebook marketing decided to focus on helping people over the age of 50 to create and build their Facebook profiles and communicate with their grandkids and friends on their Facebook wall. He wrote a book on the topic and created different educational products specifi-

cally designed for this age group. He built a successful business from it.

This is a good example of the previous idea. In a very crowded market with thousands of classes teaching people how to be successful on Facebook, he still made it. A product geared mainly towards the ages of 18-30, where standing out from the rest and making money doing so is very difficult, he took a service and applied it, and just by changing the age of his targeted customer, he was able to stand out and create a successful business from it.

LIFESTYLES

Every customer group has certain lifestyle elements in common. These may be the news papers or magazines they read, the web sites they browse, the radio stations they listen to, the vacation places that they prefer, etc.

Identifying these elements will give you a good understanding of your customers. You will learn what they are being influenced by, who they admire and follow, what else they need, and who else is communicating with them about similar products or different ways to fill the need that you're filling for them.

One of my clients, seller of wholesale makeup and beauty products, realized that every Monday he would be getting so many orders of certain products that he would run out of stock in the first few hours. Since he was not able to take more orders for these products, he was losing business. Trouble was that it was a different set of products that sold out every week so he couldn't prepare enough inventory in advanced.

He was frustrated and kept telling me, "I have thousands of products. Why do my customers always have to choose a few products? Why can't they buy the others things that I have in stock?"

I asked him for detailed order reports of the last three months. After a careful study, we discovered that he had a group of about 700 customers who were all buying the same items each week. He would then stock up on those items, thinking that this was the trend; only to find out that the following week that same group would buy different products (that he didn't have in stock!) After a few months of this pattern he was stocked up with lots of inventory that wasn't selling, all the while being short every week on inventory that was in demand.

Seeing that trend over a three month period, I knew that there had to be a reason for this, and that uncovering its reason would allow him to prepare in advance for what the customers would order.

I picked up the phone and called the first customer on the report, she was a wholesale customer who was reselling our products in her store. I told her that I wanted to thank her for her orders and for being a loyal customer. She was very surprised by the call and shared how much she liked shopping on the site. When I asked her what, specifically, she liked about the site, she said that the most important thing to her was that we ship the orders the same day and that they are delivered the next morning. The reason of its importance was because she knew by Monday which of the items her customers would want and she knew that our company would get those items to her by Tuesday morning.

When I asked her how she knew what her customers would ask for, her answer was, "Oh they all watch the Beauty show on Sunday night!" I took down the name of the show, wished her all the best, and put the phone down.

Three clicks of my computer mouse took me to this weekly beauty show where I watched replays of the most recent episodes. I compared this with our order data and it was clear why those 700 customers were ordering the same group of products.

Every Sunday night, the show had a beauty expert showing people how to dress stylishly by showing them a weekly combination of clothing, makeup and jewelry to wear based on the season and the latest trends. The show had built up a strong following of women who immediately bought whatever the expert recommended.

Store owners started watching the show themselves to know which items to prepare for the week.

I contacted the show's producers and offered them a deal: We would spend money with them in the form of sponsorships ads while the show would give us a list of what items would be discussed on the show. They agreed to send the list two weeks in advance, and that gave my customer enough time to stock enough inventory to handle the demand.

Three months later, the group of 700 buyers grew to 1600 buyers thanks to the advertisement that we put on *the show. Best of all, my client always has enough products to fill all orders now!*

Over the next six months we gained over a million dollars in new sales from this group, and it all started with taking the time to study and understand just one of his client groups.

You might have different groups of customers within your customer base and each one will have its own unique set of things they do and like. Your focus should be to learn as many details as possible about each customer group, and use that information to improve your product or service.

Look for Trend Changes in Your Customer's Behavior

When you analyze your customer list and their order history, look for changes or trends that happen over time. Sometimes you may notice that there is an increase of orders in a specific group of customers while another group has decreased their orders over the same time period.

There are constant changes in every industry in the way people decide what to buy and how to buy it. If you don't pay attention to it, you might lose a lot of current and future business because of it.

With a client of mine who sells expensive crystal gifts online, we noticed that customers had started calling in asking about getting discounts for larger quantity orders.

After studying the past few years of order data, we saw that over the last 6-12 months there was a huge increase in orders that came from party planners and interior designers, while at the same time there was a decrease in orders from general customers. Seemingly, general customers dropped out because sites like Amazon.com and Overstock.com sold similar items for less. However, the party planners and interior designers were looking for new and unique styles. In that my client specialized.

The challenge was that the website and the business model had been designed to sell single items to individuals, not to groups of designers who were buying larger orders. However, the fact that we learned about this new group of customers allowed us to make the right changes so that the site would appeal to designers and party planners. We created a special section on the site that had larger sets of matching items, and we announced different discount packages for larger orders. This drew more designers to the site and sales increased from this new customer group making up for the loss in sales from the individual client group.

Whom Are You Competing With?

When most people think about their competition they only have a few people in mind, like the guy a few blocks away that sells the same product or service, or the guy who opened a large store across town and keeps on advertising...

While it's true that those people do compete with you, your competition is a lot bigger and more spread out than these few people that you know. The problem is that while you are busy thinking about your closest competition, you are not aware of and paying attention to the more important 'big picture of competition.'

Let's take a look at the main 3 types of competitors:

COPYCATS

Copycats are the people doing the exact same thing as you do.

Example: You have a jewelry store, and there is another jewelry store down the block selling the same items as you do. Or, you have a website and there is another site selling the exact same line of products, and their site looks and feels the same as yours.

WHOLESALERS

Wholesales come in different forms. Using our example of a jewelry store, a wholesaler could be anyone of the following:

- A wholesaler that has decided to open its doors to the public and sell directly to the end user at wholesale prices.

- A large chain store that sells the same items as you do, but attracts a larger audience by selling other similar items like perfume and makeup.

- Websites like Amazon.com or Bluenile.com that sell the same jewelry that you do for better prices and with more selection than you have.

MARKET CHANGERS

Your biggest competitors are market changers. These are groups of people or companies that keep creating different solutions to the problem that your product is solving, and by doing so they are taking away your customers' needs to buy your product.

In our example of the jewelry store, a market changer would be any of the following:

A store that's selling a new type of costume (imitation) jewelry which looks the same as yours but sells for 80% less than your real jewelry:

You might think that they are not competing with you since they are not selling the same thing and a person who wants real jewelry would not be satisfied with a copy of the real thing.

That's not true! You have to assess the need that buying jewelry fills and then look if that need can be filled with imitation or costume jewelry. People buy jewelry because they want to feel good about themselves; for most people, as long as the jewelry looks real, that's enough for them to feel good.

There will always be those who only want to buy the real thing and are willing to pay the price, but that market is a very small percentage of the overall jewelry market. While you could be successful by being the best choice for the small group of customer who wants to pay the price for real jewelry, you would have to focus and build your brand to appeal to that market.

A fashion store that sells clothing and accessories:

You might not look at them as competitors, but in a way they are since they are solving the same need to feel good. The better a job they do at making people believe that their products will satisfy the need to feel good, the less people will come to your store seeking your product as the solution.

Create a list of all the different competitors you have and write down the details in which ways they are competing with you. Having this information in front of you will help you make the right decisions when it comes to purchasing or manufacturing your products or adding new services.

Kodak and Fuji were once the world's leading manufacturers and suppliers of photographic film. They looked at other film manufactures as their competition, not realizing that their biggest competition were the companies selling digital photo printing, which slowly took over the industry and forced Kodak into bankruptcy.

What's Changing in Your Industry?

Every industry is changing...

There will always be changing of trends and you have to watch for these: New products or new solutions, new customer behavior, etc.

Sometimes these changes develop over time; sometimes they can change overnight with a major invention from a large company or by a celebrity who brings awareness to a new product or style.

You want to keep reading and be informed about changes and developments in your industry. Keeping up with information provided by trade publications and online sites that are trusted in your industry will inform you of changes in key areas such as regulations, new products and services, new players in the field, recent studies, changing trends that affect demand and customer behavior, and much more. You want to keep current on what's new in your industry and where it's headed.

POINTS TO REMEMBER!

- Be clear on where you are right now
- Know your numbers
- Know your customer better than they know themselves
- Stay on top of changes in your industry
- Know your competition, but don't follow them

Chapter 2

WHAT DO YOU WANT?

Why?

As humans, we all have a deep desire to be happy and successful. We all want financial stability along with peace of mind. Throughout history, humans have strived to accomplish 'happiness' and 'success', yet very few people actually achieve these. The question is, why?

Most of us have experienced setting out to achieve goals. Whether the goals were little or large, whether they seemed difficult or even impossible – we have committed ourselves and persisted until we achieved our desired goal.

However, when it comes to success and happiness – both of which are important goals most of us strive to achieve – we seem to get lost along the way. We look in the mirror and we keep asking, "Why can't I just dowhat it takes to succeed?" No matter how many times we try, though, somewhere along the way we get stuck. We lose ourselves until we are, all over again, back at the starting point of our search for success and happiness.

The reason for this phenomenon is very simple: We work hard to achieve success but use the wrong approach. And because we are using the wrong approach, the harder we work on it the more likely it is that we will NOT achieve it.

When I ask people what they want, the answer, in most cases, would be: "I want to succeed. I don't want to stay where I am now and keep struggling with no cash flow in the bank. Do you know how difficult it is to get up every day and struggle to pay the bills? I can't go on like this for too long..."

When I interrupt them in saying that they are telling me what they **don't** want while I am looking for what they **do** want to happen, they will think for a moment and say: "I want to have enough money in the bank so that I don't have to think about it all day long. Because right now it's very hard, every day I am struggling...." And there they go right back to telling me what they don't want...

Most people have gotten into the habit of thinking in negative terms: what they don't want to happen, and what they didn't like about what did happen. Let me explain why this is a problem.

The reason why most people don't succeed in life is because they know exactly what they ***don't*** want. They keep thinking about it, focusing on it and feeling the negativity of that bad, sad thing. The more they focus their thoughts on what they don't want, the more they stay stuck in that situation because the brain is focused on it. This cannot change until they change their attitude and think about what they **do** want.

Indeed, successful people know exactly what they want and that's where their focus is. They might use the knowledge of what they don't want as a ***starting point*** to determine what they do want, but once they decide what that is they will drop the negative part of their thinking and focus on what they do want until they get it.

As human beings we are thinking all the time. Our brains are like popcorn machines that churn out thoughts nonstop. We can't 'not think', because in order to do so we must think about not thinking and that, too, is a thought process.

Experts are still researching to identify how many thoughts per minute the average person has. (Don't try to count yours – that slows down your thinking in order to make room for your counting. Your numbers won't be accurate!) It is estimated that, on average, we have one thought per second, which totals 60 thoughts per minute. That makes for 3600 thoughts per hour and a total of 43,200 in a twelve-hour day. (When we're asleep, our thoughts do not work the same way.)

Since we think in pictures, every thought creates a picture in our mind. Were our minds to be a digital camera, our 60 thoughts per minute would fill up a 2GB memory card every single minute.

Our thoughts come naturally, but between one thought and the next, a space of time occurs. We can use that tiny space to shift our thought process towards a desired direction, but it is difficult to control our thoughts, as they are a natural process.

We will explore beliefs in more detail in Chapter 3. For now, let's just say that everything we do begins with a thought which we then translate into action (to do or not to do), which then propels our actions in life, for better or for worse.

Every thought we have is either positive or negative. There are no neutral thoughts. When we have a thought we always have energy attached to it, and that energy can be positive or negative.

For example, when we think about not having enough money in our bank account and not being able to pay our bills, there will be a negative feeling attached to those thoughts. But if, for example, someone has stolen our debit card and we know that the thief won't get much money because the account is empty, that may lead to a thought with a positive feeling attached! Of course that would be temporary, as our underlying thoughts would remain negative: Not only are we broke, but our bankcard has been stolen, too! This leads to fear (definitely a negative thought) and concern about how the situation and its implications will affect us.

Most people have mainly negative thoughts. Even when a positive thought such as imagining a vacation occurs, a negative energy remains attached. Why? Although our inner images may be positive ones – such as relaxing on the beach – our inner dialogue differs. Most people quickly turn their thoughts to, "I *want* to go but I *can't* afford it," or "I *want* to go but what if things don't work out well – like my friend that missed his plane or my sister who had non-stop rain?"

Usually, our thoughts focus either on things that we have and we don't want them, or on things that we do want but don't have. The challenge with this negative way of thinking is that the mind can't operate positively when it gets negative commands. In order for the mind to help you achieve something, you have to tell it what you *do* want, and keep focusing on that until you get it. If you tell the mind what you *don't* want, you will keep getting the things that you desperately don't want to get.

> "Just because you're miserable doesn't mean you can't enjoy your life."
>
> Annette Goodheart

Don't Think About Pink Elephants

A famous example of this theory is to try not to think about pink elephants for one full minute. You will find it impossible to do. The reason is that in order for the brain not to think about pink elephants it has to think about pink elephants. By trying to push all thoughts of pink elephants aside and focus on something else, your brain will naturally keep bringing the pink elephants back into the picture while telling you not to think about them.

About 75% of the time will be spent thinking about pink elephants and 25% of this time will be spent trying not to think about pink elephants. The result is that 100% of the time will be spent thinking of pink elephants!

Another great example is seen in the world of racecar driving; in the way drivers are taught to make a sharp curve at high speeds without hitting the track wall. The only way to do this successfully is to focus beyond the curve. Racecar drivers are trained to focus on where they are heading. They are taught to ignore the wall completely, because the second they think about that wall, even if it is to think about not wanting to hit it, they will hit it. That's because there's no time to tell the brain, "See that wall? Don't *hit it.*" As this thought occurs, your body will only pick up the command in that sentence which is *hit it*, and you will. But by thinking about the road ahead, where you do want to go, your actions will take you there smoothly and safely.

When Richard Bandler, NLP founder, studied the world's top golfers to understand what they think and do to achieve success, he learned a great deal. He noticed that before these pros hit the ball they would look up and far off into the horizon. When Bandler asked them what they were looking at, they said it was nothing. But he knew differently. He could see that they were envisioning something specific. He soon realized that they were looking up and creating a picture of the hole that they wanted to drive the golf ball to. They visualized the path of the ball and saw it reaching its target. They did so even when they couldn't see the target hole from their current position.

Bandler pushed the pros to identify what they were thinking at that moment. It seemed that they were not consciously aware of what they were doing; this visualization was natural to them and happened automatically. Later, this idea was used to train new players and it proved to be a successful strategy.

A Vision Keeps You Focused

If you study the biographies of successful people in business, sports, the arts, or just about any field, you will find that all of them had a clear vision of what they wanted. And they always held strong to this vision until they achieved it.

Creating a compelling clear vision of your future gives you a positive energy to focus on; every time you think about your vision and your future you will get a positive vibration in your body, and that positive energy will keep you motivated until you reach your goal.

Let's look at two additional benefits of having a clear compelling vision:

You expect to win. Thinking about your future vision in a positive sense and seeing the end result as if you've already achieve it will send a message to your brain that you are serious about it and you expect to get there. Your brain will then give you the right thoughts and ideas to help you achieve your vision.

It helps surmount obstacles. Part of the journey of achieving anything important in life is about overcoming the hindrances along the way. You will always bump into obstacles small and large, and you must be persistent in overcoming them until you arrive at your destination. That is an integral part of any journey to success and happiness.

A clear vision and the determination to do whatever it takes will give you the courage and strength to overcome setbacks and roadblocks. When you keep your eye on your vision, you can look at any obstacle and your mind will positively ask, "How can I overcome this and move ahead in my journey, towards my vision?"

A vision is like a destination address programmed into a global positioning navigation system. Your mind is like a GPS: it navigates the route to get you to your intended destination in spite of twists and turns, blocked roads and dead-ends.

> *"Obstacles are those frightful things you see when you take your eyes off your goal."*
>
> Henry Ford

Have you ever received any of the following messages from the GPS in your vehicle?

- Due to the rain I will not be working today
- Due to the possibility of accidents on one of the roads, let's not even start
- It will take you 36 hours to get from New York to Florida. Do you think it's worth it?

Your GPS will not offer any such messages. As long as there is a clear destination input, it will consistently find the best way to get there – no matter the obstacles. If you keep following the directions provided, you will get to your destination. Because your GPS never gives up, it will simply recalculate your route from the current position and provide you with a new way of reaching it.

If you don't have a clear end-point programmed into your GPS, though, it will find it impossible to guide you at all – no matter how badly you DON'T want to stay at your current location. There is no option to program the GPS with "I have to get away from here, I don't like where I am now, take me somewhere better."

> *"If you don't know where you are going, any road will get you there."*
>
> Lewis Carroll

I CAN SEE IT!

Herman was 21 years old when we interviewed his potential in a career as a financial planner. Our hiring policy provided new financial planners with training and a salary until they gained adequate commissions from their customer base.

At the conference table sat the two partners of the firm, the sales manager, and me. We each took turns asking Herman questions. At one point I asked, *"What is your vision for your future in this field – where can you see yourself in five years?"*

I like to ask this question when interviewing people because it gives me insight to their thinking. Most of the time I get a very general answer without many details. The interviewee may tell me that they want to have a large client base, or that they want to make a lot of money in residual commissions, etc. Yet the answers usually lack specifics, details and emotions. Such a response suggests that they are answering based on what they think that, logically, the five-year vision should be. They are not offering me their unique vision as they see it in their mind's eye.

It is very easy to think of your future success in general terms. It's easy to look around at successful people and create a summary of what they have in common. It is very easy to make that your menu of success. To most people this list would include a few houses, two cars, enough money in the bank to write all desired checks, social status, respect in their company and an assortment of other details, depending on their personality and community or culture.

The flaw of a general vision of success is that it will not get you very far as it exists only on an intellectual level. For a vision to manifest, you have to feel it on an energetic level. You have to see that vision in explicit detail and feel it in your body as if it was already happening.

Back to the story of Herman. He surprised us with his answer about where he saw himself in the future. He said, "In five years from now, I have my own office where I see clients. I have 12 staff members, including an accountant and an attorney to help my customers with their retirement and estate planning." He continued on, explaining in detail how his company would operate. He even included the decor of his office and the titles of each staff member.

The room fell silent. We had interviewed a lot of people over the years, but never before had we heard someone *describe a vision with so much detail and confidence. It was especially surprising to hear this from someone so young and without any business experience at all.*

After Herman left the room, one of the partners called him "nuts" for not knowing anything about the business yet and already thinking about having his own attorney and accountant on staff. I begged to differ. This business is a very difficult in the beginning, with 96% of financial planners failing within two years because there are many obstacles until a solid client base is built. The only way to get past these obstacles is to have a clear vision of where you are going, and to focus on that when the going gets tough. Since Herman had such a clear vision, I suggested we give him a chance to execute it. And so we did.

We hired him and he went to work immediately to achieve his goal. We were amazed to watch how he handled obstacles as they arose. He possessed much creativity and many brilliant ideas for finding prospects and convincing them to buy from him.

The reason behind his success in overcoming obstacles was that he saw them as opportunities to achieve his vision. His vision was so clear that he kept moving only in that direction, naturally finding creative ways around obstacles.

Three years later he moved into his own office with yearly commissions exceeding one million dollars. The next year he hired an in-house accountant. Two months later he had his in-house attorney. It has been nine years since that first meeting and last year he was 'Number One' in the company, earning more than the other 3200 financial planners.

But All I Want is Money

Sometimes, when I ask people for a clear vision of what they want their business to look like, I receive a blank stare as they tell me "All I want is to make a little money.... "

While it is true that most people want money and one of the main reasons for people being in business is to make money, it is still very hard to make that money just because you want to. The proof is that almost everyone wants money – lots of it – and very few people actually get to that. There has to be more to acquiring money than just wanting to have it.

If you study successful people you will find that almost all of them had a clear vision of what they wanted to accomplish as well as a great passion for what they did. While they did make a lot of money from their business or skill, there was a much stronger drive behind their success then the money making. You will also find that successful people would continue working their field even when they had no need for money anymore.

> *"Money is better than poverty, if only for financial reasons."*
>
> Woody Allen

Sometimes the successful person will not be aware that he had or has a vision. Because it is so natural to him, he looks at it as part of his normal thinking pat-

> *"Money is usually attracted, not pursued."*
>
> Jim Rohn

tern. Yet, when asked, he will tell you how he had a clear picture of where he is going long before his business ever existed.

The desire to have money usually has a negative emotion to it: You want to have money but you know that you don't have it. On the other hand, if you have an exciting vision that you desire to achieve and you just need money to reach that vision, you will always find the money. That's because the underlying vision that drives you is a positive energy and the need to make money is just an obstacle on the way.

I have never seen a strong vision fail because they couldn't find the money to create and reach their vision. What I HAVE seen is businesses failing due to a lack of vision.

Can you imagine Walt Disney trying to build Disneyworld simply so he could make money? Can you imagine Bill Gates thinking about reinventing the personal computer just so he could make money? Disney and Gates would never have succeeded with such an attitude – they would've given up after the first obstacle, setback or disappointment.

Walt Disney had a strong, clear vision. When the banks turned him down, he borrowed $50,000 from his life insurance policy in order to get started. At the opening of a new theme park, long after Disney had passed away, a reporter told the new Disney CEO that it was such a shame that Walt couldn't see the opening of this new park. The CEO answered: "He saw it years ago, which is why you can see it today."

All I Want To Do Is Sit On the Beach

When we are stressed out or drained from long hours of work, we may feel the need to get away from the pressures of life and do nothing. Maybe we want to sit on the beach and relax with a newspaper and a cold beer... For years, advertisers have used such images to get customers excited about their products or services. A lot of people have bought into the idea that the goal of life and the reason behind acquiring wealth is to get to point where they can do nothing.

In fact, the opposite is actually true. Nothing is more relaxing and rejuvenating than doing work you love, feeling a sense of accomplishment at the end of every day. The feeling that you did something worthwhile, something that makes a difference to the world, is energizing. And nothing is more physically and mentally exhausting than doing nothing for a long period of time.

The concept of retirement began in the early 1900's when the Factory Age was created. Large factories were built and they hired people in their 20's with a promise: If employees would work 40 hours a week for the coming 40 years, they would be rewarded with retirement where they could do nothing for the remaining years of their life. Over time, we have formed the belief that working is not something we enjoy or look forward to; it's something we have to do in order to achieve retirement.

If you look at entrepreneurs and successful people, you will find that they never retire. They may change their working style and adjust their hours to fit their older age. But they keep working. They want to work, grow and accomplish as much as they can by using their talents and skills. Forever.

On the other hand, unsuccessful people seem to look for ways to do as little as possible, making their main goal in getting to the point where they have enough saved-up money to do nothing. I am still shocked when I interview people and one of their first questions is, "How many vacation days do you guys offer?" These people may have been unemployed for a while, out of money to pay for their basic needs, and desperate for work. Nevertheless – their minds are already focused on vacation days. They want a break from doing work they don't even have yet. Why would I hire someone who is taking the job because we offer a good vacation policy, and not because they love the job and feel that they would be great at it?

You can't be successful in business unless you enjoy doing what you're doing. If you feel that you would rather not work but don't have a choice because you have bills to pay, you will end up neither working nor having money.

In today's economy, when every business is trying to cut costs, the first people to be fired are those who do not enjoy what they do. Those who only work to earn a salary are the easiest to replace.

On the other hand, those who enjoy their work and do it with passion and creativity are less expendable and will be more difficult to replace. Since passion and creativity are unique to each individual, employers know that a replacement may not have the same passion, and that replacing the initial worker will affect bottom line results.

When we feel stressed out or run down, it's wise to take a break in order to rejuvenate. That way we can return, energized, to doing what we love!

I Don't Know What I Want...

When I consult with people about their business, many of them are not comfortable discussing their vision or what motivates them, using the excuse that they don't know what they want. This may be so because many people are very closed when it comes to talking about their vision, their goals and their feelings. Those people would rather focus on hard facts, such as how to make more money.

The reality is that no business will be successful without an emotional drive behind it. To find this deep emotional drive, you must delve into those emotional areas. The discomfort such issues bring up should be the main reason of important to go in there and actually get clear with what you want.

You might find a successful person who says that they never really knew what they wanted and just kept working until they were successful. What they don't realize is that what kept them going was the clear vision in their mind, even if they had never labeled it as such. If you'd ask them why they made the decisions that they did, you will discover that they followed their inner vision.

But I've Given Up

Another reason some people claim that they don't know what they want is because they have given up on believing that they can achieve it. This creates a "do not enter" zone in their brain; an area where there exists a foggy idea of what they want and what they think will make them happy. This is an area that many can't explore since it can be very painful; sometimes it's easier to ignore the subject and get busy than to deal with the pain. This is especially true if we feel that we don't have what it takes to turn our dreams into reality.

As children we all have a very clear vision of what we want. Ask any child what they want for the holidays and they will give you a clear list: "I want an iPhone and a remote-controlled helicopter that flies up to 100 feet high. I want an electric scooter and a swimming pool in the back yard..." They know what they want and don't hold back!

As adults we also naturally have creative ideas that could serve us well in business and in life. When kids play, you can see them let their imaginations go wild; nothing will stop them. I once watched kids create a sand castle at the beach. It was a three-story-high mansion complete with various rooms, hallways and all.

After the sand mansion was finished, one of the kids realized that they had forgotten to build steps from one floor to the next. Another one of the kids jumped right in saying, "It's not a problem – we can get a helicopter to take them to any floor they want!" Another kid added, "Let's build a heliport on each porch so the helicopter can land on whatever floor they have to be!" And off they went to work.

Creativity is a natural ability we are all born with. While some of us may have a more creative mind than others, everyone has some creativity and all of us can learn how to be more original.

"I never let my school interfere with my education."

Einstein

You may have a lot of excuses to give up on your vision – but never a good reason. And it's never too late to become the person you really are.

But It's Not Realistic

As we get older we may think that we can't create what we want because we have to be "realistic." Sometimes, when we share our visions and ideas, others tell us to get back to reality and not spend so much time thinking about things that are but irrelevant.

The people discouraging us from going after our dreams are usually the ones who are close to us. They are often our parents, teachers or siblings, and they do this with good intention – they often deem it their moral obligation to focus us on reality. The problem is that they are encouraging us to get back to *their* reality.

We all have our own beliefs that we have come to accept as reality. Others' visions and beliefs can look unreal to us, so we encourage them to get back to a reality that is basically 'our' reality. The fact remains that the other person cannot succeed with a vision that's realistic from our point of view; it has to be a vision that they develop from their perspective on life.

Here is a list of well-intentioned and 'realistic' statements that we've all heard over the years:

- *I think there is a world market for maybe five computers.* - Thomas Watson, chairman of IBM, 1943

- *640K ought to be enough for anybody.* - Bill Gates, 1981

- *The Americans have need of the telephone, but we do not. We have plenty of messenger boys.* - Sir William Preece, chief engineer of the British Post Office, 1876

- *The concept is interesting and well-formed, but in order to earn better than a 'C', the idea must be feasible.* - Yale

University professor commenting on Fred Smith's paper proposing reliable overnight delivery service. Smith went on to found FedEx

- *A cookie store is a bad idea. Besides, the market research reports say America likes crispy cookies, not soft and chewy cookies like you make.* - Response to Debbi Fields› idea to build Mrs. Fields› Cookies

- Everything that can be invented has been invented. - *Charles Duell, Commissioner, U.S. Office of Patents, 1899, requesting congress to close the patent office.*

It's hard to believe that such smart people would ever have thought like that. Sometimes thinking realistically is very limiting. Can you imagine where we would be today if everyone had accepted those statements as facts? Thank goodness most people didn't.

Better to be safe?

As we get older, we sometimes give up on our creativity and on our ability to create and execute a vision. We may begin buying into the belief that it's best to be safe and do what everyone else is doing because it's not worthwhile to "rock the boat."

The challenge with this approach is that while doing what everyone else is doing might appear to be safe, it's very hard to make money and build something while doing what everyone else does. Besides, there will

> *"I don't know the key to success, but the key to failure is trying to please everybody."*
>
> Bill Cosby

always be someone, somewhere, who will figure out a way to make the same thing you do and sell it for less. That will leave you working at a loss.

The only way to succeed is to create a vision of something that excites you. Make it something that will make a difference to others, something that will improve the way things are done, and then use your creativity to bring that vision to reality.

This does not mean that you have to invent the next online social platform or the next 'smartphone'. You can create a vision in any industry or business. It could be to improve a product or to create a unique customer experience in the way they buy or use the product, etc. It only has to be something that's better than what the market has now, and something that excites you.

I Would Be Happy To Be Like Them

Sometimes clients tell me that what they want is to be like one of their successful competitors. While it's important to know your competition, you can't use them as your guide for your business because:

- It will take you a long time to get to their level of success, and by the time you do get there, your competitor will be even further ahead. You will always be chasing after them from behind, which is never a good place to be.

- Success takes a lot of skill and effort. When a company gets something right it's because of a unique combination of skill and effort that the business team has. It is impossible for you to copy the combination that went into producing their results.

While you should learn as much as you can from successful competitors, copying them is never a good idea.

An employee of a struggling company recently told me: "My boss is watching our competitor all day long instead of building our business. For the amount of

> *"Be yourself - everyone else is taken."*
>
> Mike Robbins

time he spends watching them he might as well go work there. At least he'd get paid for his time." I couldn't have said it better.

If you look at successful companies you will see that they don't try to copy others. They went straight to the underlying need that their customers had and came up with a different, better way of addressing that need.

FedEx was not trying to copy UPS. FedEx just looked at the issues that people had in the area of shipping and created a business model to solve those issues. Apple was not trying to copy other music players or laptops. Apple changed the way we listen to music and use the Internet.

Dig as Deep as You Can

To find the passion that will keep driving you even when the going gets tough, you have to look at who you really are. Uncover the 'real you' and create a vision from there. This will ensure that your unique combination of abilities, talents and skills will be put to their best use.

Most of us have at least three different identities, and we are constantly moving from one to the other, leaving us miserable and exhausted. These are:

- **The real you** – Who you are when no one is watching, when you have no agenda, when you are relaxed, grounded and centered.

- **The Ideal you** – The person who you really want to be. This is who you believe you could be if only you knew how. Deep inside, we all have a hidden vision of what we are capable of. No matter how far we move away from our potential, this ideal version will always be there. If you don't get to fulfill this identity, you may feel that something is sorely missing.

- **The Masked identity** – This 'made- up' identity may change daily based on how you want others to perceive you. This makes you behave in line with how you think such an identity would behave. The challenge here is that living as someone else is exhausting and unfulfilling. Unfortunately, after years of putting on this masked identity, you may get so used to it that you continue with it; even if you are unhappy, you may feel stuck with this façade. You are not. The true you remains inside even when it feels that you don't know who you are anymore.

People can spend a lot of the time in their masked identity. Trying to find your passion or trying to create a vision while in a masked identity will only create a result that won't satisfy the real you.

Sometimes it can be hard to allow yourself to be. If you have adopted masked identities for a long while, the real identity may feel like strange and unfamiliar territory. This can be daunting, even frightening.

One of the best ways to uncover the 'real you' is to start with the simple question: "What do I really want?" Keep asking the same question over and over, and keep listening until you hear the real you reply.

You can build a large company, make a lot of money and see success. But if you build this using your masked identity it won't last. The real you does not have the skills to manage the temporary success achieved. Even if you do maintain the money or success, you'll never feel happiness because it's not in alignment with the real you.

"I don't need to worry about identity theft because no one wants to be me."

Jay London

True Success

To succeed in business and in life, you will need:

Clear vision: The detailed sight of where you are going and how it will look like when you get there.

Persistence: The ability to keep going forward, despite the obstacles, until you reach your vision.

The only way to find both components is to dig deep within and uncover the real you, with your natural abilities and skills, then allow that person to be. From that place, you can create a compelling vision of what you want to accomplish. And from there – simply go and do it.

"Success consists of going from failure to failure without loss of enthusiasm."

Winston Churchill

It's All About Balance

Nearly every time a successful person is interviewed they are asked this question: "When looking back on your life or career, which thing would you change or do differently?" Most successful people answer, "I would have focused more time on other areas of life outside of the business." The more balanced your life the more successful you will be in business. Successful people understand this concept of balance very well, but unsuccessful people have a hard time with it.

Success is a lifelong quest that never ends. You need a strong foundation of family, friends and self-care to have the physical and mental strength to keep going and to be doing what it takes every single day to achieve success.

> "It's not the million dollars that's important; it's the person you have to become in order to earn a million dollars."
>
> Jim Rohn

Create your vision

Everything starts with a vision, which is the destination that you desire. Your vision is the driving force that will keep you going when things get tough and you bump into the obstacles along the way.

Writing a vision is simple but not always easy. All you need is a piece of paper, a pen and a few hours of uninterrupted time so that you can write a compelling vision of a life that will excite you and make you feel accomplished and fulfilled.

When you write your vision there are two important things to remember. One is that it has to be your vision not someone else's vision. We often build a vision for the future based on what we see other people have or what we think others expect our future to be like. You will not feel happy and fulfilled achieving another person's vision. It has to be your vision. It has to be something that you feel is important, something that will keep you excited to get up and work every day to achieve it.

The second thing to remember is that a vision does not have to be realistic. Write down whatever comes to mind. If you stop to think what is logical, you will end up with a small vision based on who you currently are, rather than a vision for the person who you will become. A small vision will not be exciting to work on and will not be fulfilling when you achieve it, so let your dreams go wherever they like and keep writing as if you are not responsible to achieve it.

You want to make sure that your vision covers all four major categories of life: spiritual, physical, family and financial. Focusing only on one or two areas and ignoring the rest will create an imbalanced life. You might end up being miserable in the area you ignored, so you want to make sure that you cover all four categories in your vision.

REVERSE LOOKUP

Once you have your vision written down, it's time to move on to the next step of making it happen. You want to start by visualizing your life as if you are living your vision. Get into the feeling of it, see it in full color and get your body into the feeling. Enjoy and savor how it all feels and sit with the feeling for a few minutes.

Then look back and follow the path you took to get there. Start at the end and look for the last actions you took. Slowly walk your way backwards. Visualize all the action you took to arrive at your vision, as well as the obstacles and setbacks you've encountered along the way. Picture how you handled them all.

Once you can see the path that you took, take your pen and write down all the steps and actions that you will take to achieve your vision.

CREATING YOUR TIMELINE

Set a time in the future when you will achieve your vision. Then create smaller goals that you will achieve along the way. Build in rest areas along the way so that you can stop and feel accomplished knowing that you are on the right track.

> *"As you climb the ladder of success, check occasionally to make sure it is leaning against the right wall."*
>
> Author Unknown

You want to have yearly goals and then split them up into monthly goals. Make sure that your yearly and monthly goals cover all four areas of your life to keep your progress towards your vision balanced.

Write down your goals for the next 12 months in each of the four areas:

1. Spiritual _____
2. Physical _____
3. Financial/career _____
4. Family/personal _____

POINTS TO REMEMBER!

- Keep your focus on what you want, ignoring what you don't want.
- Your mind can't work with negative commands.
- Money by itself is not a goal worth pursuing.
- Be yourself.
- Create a compelling vision and keep your focus on it.

Chapter 3

WHAT'S STOPPING YOU?

He Wants You To Succeed

Now that you have a clear vision, let's take a look at the things that can stop you from achieving your goals and how to deal with them effectively. In order to make any changes to our lives and businesses, we have to have a good understanding of how things happen and how we create our own reality. Understanding this concept will change your life forever. It will give you the insight and the tools needed to change your reality when you don't like where you are. It will help you achieve anything you would like to achieve.

Before we get into the details, I would like to clarify a topic that confuses many people and some people use as an excuse for not doing anything. It is about the Will of God.

Many people feel that since if God wants us to succeed we will – regardless of what we do – there should be no reason to work hard towards succeeding since it all depends on the Will of God. This tune is sung by many and adopted as an excuse for people to stay where they are stuck. They may stay at a job that pays minimum wage thinking that if God really wants them to be rich He will make them a way. They may fantasize that the boss will increase their pay from minimum wage to partnership, or perhaps that they will win the lottery or find a treasure.

The truth is that God plans everything that happens to us in life, big or small. Whatever He does is for our benefit and everything is in alignment with our mission on this world. So, there is no reason to be concerned about what happened yesterday: All that happens to us is meant to happen and is for our own good. The future has been predetermined in great detail, and it will unfold as it is supposed to. We need not worry about that either.

But, and this is a big BUT. At the present moment, YOU have a responsibility to do whatever you can to succeed. You must put your best effort forward in order to achieve your potential. God gave you free will; your choices will affect your results.

Have you heard this story about a lotto ticket? A man is in big trouble; he has no income and is in huge debt. He prays, "Please, God, help me win the lottery so that I'll be able to pay off my debts and provide food for my family."

Nothing happens. So the next day he prays again. "Please, God, I promise to be good, to follow all your rules, will you just help me win the lottery."

A few more days pass with no positive results. The man's anxiety keeps growing. Again, he prays. "God, I am running out of options. Please help me win the lottery before it's too late."

Suddenly he hears a voice from above: "Would you do me a favor and buy a lottery ticket!"

I strongly believe that God wants you to succeed. He has given you ideas to formulate what you can do to contribute to your success. He even arranged for this book to get into your hands! He wants you to take action, to use your innate talents and skills, to follow your desires and to make both your world as well as the larger world a better place.

Will you?

> *"Our deepest fear is not that we are inadequate. Our deepest fear is that we are powerful beyond imagination."*
>
> Marianne Williamson

We Create Our Own Reality!

What we get in life is a result of our choices of action or lack of such; either way we make choices that result in the outcome we know as reality.

Let's look at an example:

I met David a few months ago. His complaint was that sales were down. When I asked him why he thinks sales are down he said, "We are in a recession and people are just not buying like they used to." What David was really telling me was that he believes that his current reality is a result of an outside factor – the recession. Since outside factors are beyond his control, there is nothing that he can do about it.

I asked David: "Why don't you add more services/products to increase sales and make up for those lost by recession?" He told me: "You can't do that. It wouldn't work!"

My next question was: "Can you hire more sales people to expand your client base and make up for lost sales?" He answered: "I have tried that years ago and it didn't work out."

Next was: "What can we change to make your product/service unique in order to make it stand out from the crowd and so create more demand for it?" His answer was: "There is nothing unique. We are all selling the same thing. Trust me, I`ve been in this industry for 25 years and I know that it's all the same."

Looking at these answers, would you say that David's sales are partially a result of his thinking and his inaction?

From his answers, it is very clear that his beliefs and assumptions are holding him back from taking the right steps to increase his sales. He believes that he is doing everything he can and that his reality is just the way it is because of circumstances beyond his control.

Imagine someone building a jail cell and then sitting inside it for years. Imagine this person telling himself and those around him how much he wished he could leave his cell and have his freedom. Imagine others telling him that there is no **real** jail here and that he **can** leave any time he wants but that he simply cannot understand.

In some ways we have all created our own personal jails, the walls of which consist of our limiting beliefs we have accepted as facts. We operate inside those cell walls believing that it's impossible to get out.

We all have our own limitations that differ from person to person depending on our beliefs. So we all build a slightly different jail cell. But everyone operates within his own cell walls, believing that he can't move beyond.

When we look at this analogy from the outside it doesn't make sense. How can so many people build a prison out of their beliefs, while those same issues are not a problem for others?

As with anything else, it`s easy to see things clearly when we look at someone else's situation. When we look at our own reality it`s hard to see it clearly and accept the fact that we have created it. Harder still is to believe that we have the ability to change it.

So, my question to you is this: "If it is true that you can create your own reality and live your full potential, when would you like to know about it?" Would now be a good time?

How We Create Our Reality

We are constantly making decisions – what we should or should not do. These actions create the results that shape our reality. All you see as you look at your life today is a result of your previous actions as well as the importance you gave them.

For example, let's say you sleep in late. That could result in you being fired, which could result in you not being able to pay your bills, which could result in a lot of stress and unhappiness. Losing your job and the subsequent lack of money were a result of your action of sleeping in late. The stress and unhappiness are a direct result of your decision to sleep late.

When we hear the alarm clock go off in the morning, we have a thought about the importance of getting up right now and make it to work on time. We may also have another thought about the importance of sleeping another hour. We then have to make a decision which thought is really more important, and that decision will result in our action of getting up or not, which will shape our reality for the day and the future.

A decision is the end result of a thought. We think about an issue or something that we want, and that thought turns into action to either do something or not to do. The thoughts happen automatically – about 60 times per minute – constant decisions are being made, shaping the reality we are experiencing.

Where Do Thoughts Come From?

We all have different, unique ways of looking at and thinking about any situation.

Five people can look out the window in the morning and see snow; each one of them will have an automatic chain of thought, and they will be different from one another.

Person 1: What a beautiful scene! Thank God for snow! This is so peaceful and relaxing. I'm going to get a cup of tea and enjoy the view.

Person 2: I can't believe this. The last thing I need today is snow! It's my bad luck. What can I do, nothing goes the way I want.

Person 3: Wow, this is a lot of snow; we're going to have so much fun in it. Let's take the day off from work and go skiing. We could use a break from work anyway.

Person 4: I love to walk in the snow. I'm going to leave the car at home today and walk to work! Oh, maybe some people won't make it to the office today; I'll go in early to help out.

Person 5: What a mess! I bet it will take them a week to clean all this snow up. And the garbage will pile up. Oh, the house will get so dirty from people coming in with wet boots. What about my delivery? What if UPS can't deliver my package today and I lose that order! That's it, I've had enough, we are moving to Florida.

Each one of these people will now take actions based on those thoughts, and all action will be different from one another. How is it possible that five people look at the same picture but each get onto a different train of thought?

The answer is that our thoughts are being generated by our subconscious mind, which has large servers of data, including all of our beliefs and past experiences. When we look at something our subconscious mind will generate thoughts using all the relevant data it can bring up on that subject.

The two main filters the brain uses to generate thoughts are beliefs and past experiences.

How Do We Create Beliefs?

Every thought that we accept as fact becomes a belief. We add this new belief to our large database of beliefs, which then serves as the foundation for generating new thoughts.

Using our example of looking out the window and seeing snow, we see that each one of the five people already had beliefs around snow and what it means to them. While most of us have enjoyed the snow as kids, that may have changed as we grew older. Through a combination of our experiences and how we view life (beliefs), we may create a belief about snow being positive or negative. Our mind knows this association already, and it automatically generates thoughts from there.

Let's look at each one of our snow gazers and guess what their belief about snow is:

Person 1: Belief – _snow is relaxing._

Person 2: Belief – _snow creates a big mess._

Person 3: Belief – _snow is fun._

Person 4: Belief – *snow is part of nature and I love nature.*

Person 5: Belief – *snow is part of the universe's plan to keep me miserable.*

We have beliefs about everything in life. We experience life based on the decisions we make as a result of various combinations of our beliefs. We convince ourselves that the way we see things is the real and only way since it stems from the beliefs we think of as facts.

THE FOUR-MINUTE MILE

A famous example of the power of a belief is that of the 'Four-Minute Mile.' Up until 1954 it was thought that a human being could not run a mile in under 4 minutes. Some scientists even stated that the skin would explode should we run faster than that! No one even tried to beat that record since it was seen as an impossible goal.

That all changed in 1954 when Roger Bannister ran a mile in three minutes and 59 seconds. This disproved the incorrect belief about how fast humans could or could not run. By the end of 1957, sixteen people ran a mile in less than four minutes. The record was pushed down to three minutes and 50 seconds, and a new belief was born: Human beings can run faster than thought before.

But my beliefs are facts, aren't they?

How do we know if something is just a belief or is indeed a real fact? The answer is that very few things are actual facts.

Most of the things that we consider to be facts are nothing more than beliefs. They may be personal or even global beliefs that a lot of people accept as facts, but they remain only beliefs. For almost any of the beliefs that we have, there is someone out there who thinks otherwise. For years people believed it to be fact that the world was flat!

> *"The thinking that created the problem can't create the solution."*
>
> Einstein

Until 2011, we considered the speed of light as the fastest speed possible, based on Einstein's theories. In 2011, neutrinos were discovered – ghostly subatomic particles traveling faster than the speed of light. This new discovery has now removed a global belief that was considered fact. Many other beliefs in physics have been built on that belief, so they too will change.

Different Perspectives

Here is a simple exercise that I use in classes to show the power that beliefs have on our lives. I ask the audience to fill in these blanks as fast as they can:

- Life is _____
- People are _____
- Sales are _____

Then we go around the audience to hear what people wrote in the blank space. Other people are usually amazed to see how many answers there can be on the question of what life is. Below are some of the answers this exercise has generated.

	Life is ____	People Are____	Sales Are____
Person A	Wonderful	Amazing	Opportunities
Person B	Hell	Bad	Difficult
Person C	A test	Dangerous	Challenges
Person D	A Journey	Friendly	Fun
Person E	A game	Unpredictable	Uncomfortable

Let's look at the following scenarios and see how each person would act based on their beliefs.

SCENARIO ONE

It's 9am on a Monday. You are sitting at your desk, looking at your sales numbers for the month. You see that you have a long way to go to reach your minimum goal for the month. You have a list of potential prospects to call and ask for their business. What thoughts are going through your mind? What action does this spur you to? What results are you likely to get?

	Thoughts – Beliefs	Action	Results
Person A	Life is great and there are a lot of amazing people out there that I can call and ask them for business. Sales are opportunities and people are great, let's do it!	Sales calls	Great conversations with nice people and relationship building for short- and long-term sales.

	Thoughts – Beliefs	Action	Results
Person B	Life is Hell, people are bad, and selling is difficult. I hate doing this every day. Why can't my life be like...?	No action	More frustration and evidence that life is hell and selling is difficult.
Person C	Life is a test, people are dangerous and a sale is a challenge, but I am ready to take the test and win the challenge.	Sales calls	Closes some sales with people who will buy if you are persistence with them.
Person D	We are on a journey, people are nice, and sales are fun. Let's have fun.	Sales calls	Lots of sales with people who love the change in state that you give them with your positive outlook in life.
Person E	Life is a game, people are unpredictable and selling is a game, but the type of game that I don't enjoy playing.	No action	The game of life continues, and selling would probably not be part of your game.

SCENARIO TWO

You are so overwhelmed by all your daily tasks that you can't follow up or follow through. You recognize that it's time to hire a helper to take over some of your responsibilities so that you can focus on building the company instead of running the daily operations. Let's take a look at how this process would play out with our group:

	Thoughts – Beliefs	Action	Results
Person A	There are so many amazing people out there. Let's find someone good that I can give over the responsibilities, and if they succeed I will succeed as well.	Interviewed and hired a motivated, positive person to take charge of daily operations.	A successful company where daily operations run without your involvement, and you can focus on the big picture.
Person B	It's bad enough as is, now I have to hire someone who would not even be good and pay salary every week. But what can you do? That's life.	Interviewed and hired a low-pay employee full of fears who is scared to take action out of fear that they might do something wrong.	You are still doing all the work, because you can't trust the new employee since she might mess things up. And now you have more proof that for some people life is just hell. (And it doesn't even pay to try to do something about it).
Person C	This is another test; since people are dangerous, I have to be very careful with whom I bring into my company.	Lots of interviews with no one hired.	As soon as I find someone I feel I can trust, I will hire them. until then, I will keep doing it myself.
Person D	They are so many nice people out there, it will be a lot of fun to have someone here working along.	Hires the first person that comes for an interview.	Stuck with a nice employee who is incapable of running the operations.

Person E	Let's play this safe. I have to figure out a real game plan before I can bring in another person.	No action	The game of life continues, but fo r now you will be playing the game alone.

As you can see, we will take action and achieve results based on our different beliefs. We may not even notice that we have preset beliefs playing such a big role in our responses and therefore in the results we get.

Most people believe that the way they do something is the only way and the right way, and can't think of how someone would do anything differently.

If you take any belief from any of the people in the group and change it, the process and results would immediately change accordingly.

Another thing to consider in regard to varying perspectives is that a company usually consists of a group, and that group must make decisions as a whole. Each person in the group has his own unique set of beliefs and will see the situation from his unique perspective. This can be used to the advantage of the group and the company since it offers a variety of views on any given issue, and that can help in weighing the options. However, this also requires each person to understand and respect one another's views. Seeking clarity, by asking people to explain their point of view, gives everyone else the chance to see a new belief and a different perspective.

But Who Is Right?

The answer is that everyone is right. Life is what it is and you can make of it whatever you like. The same is true for people, and the same is true for sales! Everything can be good or bad depending on how you look at it and what you make of it.

Sometimes I see people go into long discussions to prove that they are right. The problem is that life does not give you points if you are right. It's irrelevant if I think you are right or

> *"War does not determine who is right – only who is left."*
>
> Bertrand Russell

wrong. The question to focus on is what needs to be done to accomplish your vision or goal.

If you are driving down the freeway and you see a car coming straight at you because he is driving in the wrong direction, you are 100% right and he is 100% wrong. But you have a critical decision to make, and fast: Do you want to be right or do you want to live? If you want to live then move over quickly!

Arguing about who is right or wrong often comes from low self-esteem or a belief that there is only one right way to do something. People sometimes feel they need the approval of others around them so that they can feel good about themselves. Approval doesn't matter, though, because the reality is that there is no right and wrong. For everything that you do, there will be some people who think it's right and some people who think it's wrong.

When they asked Donald Trump for his response to the question, "Life is like...?" he said, "Life is a game and there can only be one winner." This explains his tough negations in real estate deals as well as his general behavior to make sure he always stays the winner.

"I don't know the key to success, but the key to failure is to try to please everybody."

Bill Cosby

Who Can We Blame?

The challenge with our beliefs is that since we accept them as facts we convince ourselves that there is nothing we can do about our current situation. We may not like the way we are or the life we live, but we feel that we can't be at fault since we think that we are doing the best we can with what we have. We then start looking for outside sources to blame.

Some people will always blame the government and its policies; some people will blame the Democrats while others will blame the Republicans. It's amazing how creative people get when it comes to pointing blame! Some people blame the previous political party, claiming that current problems are because of what they did when they were in control.

Who is right? Who cares?

While some people may argue about who is to blame for a bad economy, for example, others believe that they can make money in any economy, no matter who is running congress, and they do!

"Those who say it can't be done are usually interrupted by others doing it."

James Arthur Baldwin

The problem with blaming is that it shifts the focus of the brain away from finding opportunities and solutions. It creates a victim mentality, where you don't feel the need to do anything since you don't think that the problem is your fault and therefore you are not responsible for the solution.

The brain is an amazing organ. If you give it a clear task it will find ways to get anything done, no matter how challenging. It will do so by asking questions like "How do I get there? What can I do today that will get me closer to my vision?" However, your brain will only do this when you are 100% clear about what you want to achieve and are determined that you WILL achieve it. This is when the brain will get to work, helping you achieve the entire world.

But if you are not determined in achieving your vision, then the question to the brain is not, "How do I get there?" The question turns into "Can I get there?" or "Should I even get there?" This series of thoughts will have you going in circles, never moving towards a solution. Because the brain will keep giving you excuses why now is not the right time to focus on your vision.

I n January of 2008 I was hired by a large commercial loan brokerage firm in NYC to help their sales people set goals for the new year. The firm had 62 sales reps – all of them commission-based.

The first person I met was the top sales person in the company. As we began discussing his plans for the new year he said: "Last year I earned 9.4 Million dollars in commission, I am not sure how much higher I can go this year since we are in a down housing market and the banks are not lending money to investors. But I am confident that I can close enough big deals that I can earn over 10 million in commissions in 2009. Do you think that's a reasonable goal?"

I told him that it was very reasonable and suggested that we get to work on an action plan that will hold him accountable to reach his goal. We designed a clear plan for his daily and weekly prospecting and marketing in order to find the right deals for him.

Three days later I met with one of the lowest producers in the company. When I asked him what his goals were for the new year his reply was: "I'm not sure. Last year I made about $38,000 in commission, but now we are in a down market, so I don't think I can reach that number this year. Is it ok if I set my goal at $30.000, just to be on the safe side? Do you think that's reasonable?"

On my way home I realized that over the last three days two different people had asked me if their goals were reasonable, but there was 9.7 million dollar difference between the two! Both of them worked for the same company and had the same opportunities but one of them believed it's reasonable to earn 10 million while the other believed it reasonable to earn $30,000.

It was obvious to me that the only difference between these two employees was their belief system: One believed that many opportunities were available in the marketplace and that he would find them and earn 10 million dollars. The other believed that there were no deals available and that he doesn't have what it takes to find the few deals in a down market.

That little difference in their belief had a big effect on their thoughts and actions all year long. Every morning one of them would get up knowing that today he would make progress in getting large deals, while one of them would get up knowing that today would be another recession day where not much would get done. The events of each day would reflect those beliefs and the cycle would continue.

POINTS TO REMEMBER!

- God wants you to succeed but you have to put in the effort.
- You create your own reality.
- Our reality is a result from our decisions.
- Our decisions come from our thoughts which are generated by our beliefs.
- Take responsibility for your success.

Chapter 4

CHANGE YOUR MIND

Change Your Mind and Your Results Will Follow

If everything that we have in life originates from our belief system, it would make sense to conclude that changing our beliefs would automatically change our results and our reality.

Changes in belief can happen. For example, as you read this book you will find your beliefs starting to shift. You may now see that facts are usually beliefs we have created. You may now look at situations differently. You may identify your central belief about the situation and ask yourself, "Is it possible that if I change my belief, the results will change?"

You don't have to answer that question. By simply looking at your automatically triggered belief, you are accepting the possibility that another perspective may be possible. The thought will generate new ideas, which will lead to new actions. If these actions bring you your desired result, your new thoughts will be reinforced. You will have created a new and more positive belief.

Every time you see a story about someone who made a major change in their life, you will see that they had a major shift in their belief system. And from that point on, everything was different for them.

Sometimes it is pain that convinces us that there has to be a better way of living than the way we are now. That simple shift in belief starts us on the path of finding a better way.

One of my friends who worked at Bear Stearns had such a moment. As a highly paid employee with the company for years, he believed that he had to put his all into his work, build up a large portfolio of company stock and climb the corporate later to the highest position possible.

In 2007, when the troubles began for Bear Stearns, he started questioning his belief in the company. For the first time ever, it crossed his mind that maybe he had put too much importance into his work and had neglected other areas of his life.

On March 16, 2008, he awoke to the news that the U.S government had forced a merger with JP Morgan Chase, who bought Bear Stearns for $2 per share. That meant that his accumulated portfolio of 80,000 shares in the company stock fell from $13.7 million ($172 per share) to $160,000 ($2 per share) in less than a year. Having spent his days, nights and weekends working to achieve his high position, he was now reduced to a minor manager with a small portfolio.

The next day he got an offer from JP Morgan Chase to keep his position and salary in the newly merged company. He said no, and left the corporate world. He decided to devote himself to learning God's teachings and to charity.

When we met a few months later I asked him to share what went through his mind in those tumultuous 2 days.

He explained that he had felt extremely lost, not because he was afraid of his job (he did have savings!), but because his foundation of beliefs of what's important in life was shaken. He no longer knew what was important.

Until then, he has had a very clear set of beliefs that gave him a solid foundation to base decisions on. But that day he looked out his office window trying to absorb what was happening and that was the turning point of his life. When he now thinks about the collapse of the business, their bankruptcy and forced merger, his loss of status and wealth – he isn't bothered. He now has a new set of beliefs that allow him to see that there are things in life more important than businesses and money. Now he is happy that he learned such a valuable life lesson. He now looks forward to spending his time doing things that are a lot more important than working.

When he got the offer from JP Morgan Chase to stay with the new company, he didn't have to think about it. His decision was clear: he was no longer interested in working. His new set of beliefs had already generated new thoughts that helped him make a firm decision. He now has new results and a new life.

Creating A Balance

It is important to stress that whenever we make changes in life, we want to make sure that we consider all the important areas in life. You can't just focus on one area while neglecting the other areas.

You can't be balanced at work while you are unbalanced in your personal or religious life, because they work together. A lack in one area will pull down the other areas.

> *"Money often costs too much."*
>
> Ralph Waldo Emerson

If you are not healthy or your family life is a mess, it will affect your work even if you have your business goals planned out in detail.

"How are you?"

Consider the wide range of answers to this question. From "totally messed up" to "amazingly well" is a wide range of options in how we assess our mood or our quality of life to be.

Most of us feel that we fall somewhere in the middle of the range: we are not as bad as others are, but we are also not as good as some people are. Sometimes that mid-range is not such a good place to be. In that space there can be a lack of enthusiasm to do something because we may just be trying to keep "not so bad" things from getting worse. This space can leave us unmotivated to take charge and create the extraordinary life that we want and deserve. The result is that we do not reach the true potential we have.

Many people are afraid to say that they are doing amazingly well, because it just doesn't sound right. After all we still have a list of things that we need or want but don't have. Many people fear that admitting to being "amazing" would mean that they admit that they don't want or need anything else. That can make some people feel that they are accepting that they are amazingly happy to be wherever they are. And that would be just terrible...

How do we measure how well we are doing in life? Most people try to base this on their vision of what they want to have, what they want to be and how they want to feel. But when we are not there yet – we don't have what we want, are not who we want to be, and do not feel the way we want to feel – we usually can't measure ourselves worthily. This makes us measure ourselves at the "so-so" or "okay" level of the 'how I'm doing' scale.

Yet, in order to grow in any area of life, we need to be strong and feel amazing. It is this strength and optimism that will make us continue taking the necessary steps in order to keep growing.

The truth is that we are all perfect human beings created by God. So, in truth, we are always amazing and doing very well in our many different roles, and we have to keep growing in each one of them every day. The combination of our work and growth in all those areas will help us reach our potential, serve the world and serve God in a way that's unique to each one of us.

One of the best ways to look at life is that you have different roles that you need to perform to the best of your ability. You might be a son, a father, a brother, an employer, a friend, a community volunteer, a religious person, etc.

To keep striving and growing in each of your life roles is all you can do. You can't control the outcome of events, so the only obligation to yourself is to do your best. Sometimes you might do everything right and still not achieve what you want. You can't always predict your outcomes, but you can do your best every day. That way you know that you put in your maximum effort and that's what matters.

Of course, your roles will change as you age. When you have your first child you have a new role as a father and you must learn and work every day to be the best father you can. You will have a lot of challenges and you will keep growing and learning.

There is no scoreboard to compare how you are doing against everyone else; we are all different and unique. You will only feel happy and successful when you do your best with life and with the challenges it brings.

Even as an employer you might have different roles. For example, if you run your own small business, you might have to be the bookkeeper, secretary, sales manager, marketing manager, operations officer, buying officer, etc. You will keep learning and working everyday to improve these skills. It's a never-ending game, and as long as you are playing the game to the best of your ability, you are a winner.

Your Roles

Write down your top ten roles in life:

1) I am a ....

2) I am a ....

3) I am a ....

4) I am a ....

5) I am a ....

6) I am a ....

7) I am a ....

8) I am a...

9) I am a...

10) I am a...

Now go back and take each role and find one belief that you have in regard to that role.

For example:

Role #1) *I am a father.*

Belief: *I have no idea what the right way to raise my kids is.*

Role #2) ....

Belief ....

Role #3) ....

Belief ....

Role #4) ....

Belief ....

Role #5) ....

Belief ....

Role #6) ....

Belief ....

Role #7) ....

Belief ....

Role #8) ....

Belief ....

Role #9) ....

Belief ....

Role #10) ....

Belief ....

You now have 10 beliefs that are affecting your results in those areas of your life – together they are creating the reality you are experiencing. If you don't like the results that you are getting in this area then you might want to consider a change of belief.

If you find yourself reading along without doing the exercise in writing, that's fine, but know that it always helps to write things down. Writing it down reinforces your beliefs and becomes part of your thinking process. Regardless of what you do here, changes in belief are happening automatically as you read through.

Change is Easy

If you have a belief that change is difficult, then that belief makes change difficult. So let's change this belief first.

Change, by definition, is very easy: You stop doing one thing and you start doing another. The reason why most people find change difficult is because of the negative emotions [mainly fear] that we attach to it. Also, most people like the comfortable familiarity of what they know and fear going into unfamiliar territory even if it benefits them.

Most business owners I've met say things like, "My employees are a liability to my company. I wish I could do without them and save all that payroll money." If you realize that this is just a thought, not a fact, and that there are alternative thoughts like "Every employee is an asset to the company and my job is to help them develop their unique skills and abilities to create bigger value to the company and to the marketplace", then you have more positive possibilities. Even if you don't accept the thought quite yet, you will look at your employees differently. That will affect your decisions and how well your business does.

You want to consider the following points:

- Each employee is an asset to your company because they contribute to its overall success. The success of any company is a combined effort of all its people and parts working together in harmony.

- It is impossible for you to build or run a successful company by yourself. You are just one person and cannot be skilled at everything that needs to be done. Your employees fill the missing parts, and that turns them into great assets.

- A lot of creativity and new ideas within successful companies come from employees who care about the success of the company. This makes them an important factor to the long-term success of your company.

Keep thinking about these points and your mind will naturally adopt the new belief and start generating thoughts and actions with the new understanding of employees being an asset. Do that, and you will soon find yourself seeing and treating them as the assets they really are.

One the best rewards in coaching companies is when a business owner tells me, "I am not sure what exactly you did, but the environment in the office is a lot better since you came. People are more excited to work and they work together as a team..."

The reason this is happening is my talking to the owner for hours, helping him change his beliefs. Without even knowing it, he starts to act differently towards his employees. He appreciates them more and they feel it. This gets them excited about their work and creates a much better atmosphere in the business.

It's Easier To Succeed Than To Fail

Some people have a belief that it's hard to succeed since it takes a lot of work, while failing is easy because you don't have to really do anything!

The reality is that you are actually working quite hard to fail. If you just decide to change attitude and head in the direction of success, you'll find that it's far easier to succeed than it is to stay in the state of losing.

Let's imagine for a minute that you decided to take a six-month vacation to get away from everything. Let's say that I'm supposed to take over all your responsibilities, maintain your business and manage your life. In order for me to do this you will have to teach me exactly how to be you and how to do all of the things you do. You have to teach me what to think and what to say as well.

For example, let's say that you have a small business selling office supplies. Let's say you are struggling to make ends meet; you have just enough money to get through this week's payroll. Every Monday you have to start the struggle again, figuring out how to get new sales and new cash flow into the system.

Now you have to teach me how to do this for the next six months, remember. Let's say that you told me to start every morning by looking at the bank balance to ensure that all checks went through; then checking if any orders came in overnight; spending the day waiting for orders; checking stock to see if those orders can be filled; placing an order with your supplier if those orders can't be filled, and then invoicing the customer.

You let me keep doing this for six months and you hope that nothing goes wrong. Frankly, a few things go wrong every week, but you hope for the best.

Now I have a few questions for you: Can I call previous customers to see if they need anything? Can I create a special sales offer and email-blast all customers in your database? Can I hire a salesperson on commission? Can I add more items to your current line of inventory?

You answer might be that I could do all those things, but it's possible that the customers who I call will not have anything to order, and some of them might even be upset why I am calling them.

You may approve that I create an email with a special sales offer but then think you will make less profit this way. Still, you never know who might order without having to use any offers.

You may agree to let me look for a salesperson on a commission basis, but you might suggest that someone like that will be hard to find since they all want salary, and even if I do find someone it would mean you losing some profits due to the commissions paid to the salesperson.

You may agree to add more products and expand the current line, but say that would cost you more in inventory without you being sure that your customers would buy the new products.

So, in order for me to replace you, I have to accept the following beliefs:

- Calling customers is not a good idea
- Neither is emailing them specials
- Looking for a salesperson to work for commission is a waste of time and a unworthy project
- Adding more products is too risky

The more time you spend teaching me how to replace you, the more you will realize that you work hard every day to stay stuck in your current position. Your beliefs make you struggle to make ends meet.

You have been doing things the same way for so many years that it looks and feels natural to you. Remember that it takes a lot of work every day to stay in a position of failure. Changing your limiting beliefs and negative habits into new and empowering ones that will help you achieve success is not easy at first. We have to change something familiar to us into something that is unfamiliar. As soon as we break through the first few weeks, however, it will actually be easier to do the things that will make us successful than it was to do the things that kept us in failure.

When we look at someone else and how they are running their life and business, it's easy to see how their beliefs and actions are keeping them stuck in their current situation. It can also be easy to see that if they would only change a few things, they could succeed.

But when it comes to our own life, we are convinced that we do whatever we can to succeed. We are sure that our beliefs are actual facts. We like to feel that we are good people and it would be hard to accept the fact that we are responsible for our success or lack of it.

All it takes is the decision to get off your current road to nowhere and start down the road to success. Create new beliefs and habits, enforce them with actions, and you will create a new reality for yourself. Success will come be the natural result.

But....

Beware when that little voice in your head starts up and questions your intent to change something in a direction where the results are unknown and will take you out of your comfort zone.

The voice in our head operates out of fear. Although it seems to be trying to keep us safe, it is in fact crippling us by keeping us stuck with our old beliefs. This fearful and protective voice may tell you:

➢ Why rock the boat, leave everything the way it is

➢ Don't take chances, you never know what can happen

➢ It's bad now, but it might get worse, so don't risk it

➢ If you start looking at your employees as an asset, they might take advantage of it and ask for a raise

The voice in your head will do whatever it can to keep you where you are – regardless of whether that place is good for you or not and regardless of whether the mutterings make sense or not.

If you really want to change your life and your business, listen to the thoughts of this voice. Then realize what it's trying to do. It wants to keep you stuck in the place of familiarity and comfort. Don't ignore the voice, and don't argue with it. Just notice it for what it is and it will disappear.

When you accept your fears for what they are, without resisting them, you will disconnect yourself from your thinking process and look at them as an external thought that does not relate to you.

Always remember that change is easy. All you need is a commitment to change. There is no need to prepare, it's free, and you can do it anytime you choose to.

> *"Inaction breeds doubt and fear. Action breeds confidence and courage. If you want to conquer fear, do not sit home and think about it. Go out and get busy."*
>
> Dale Carnegie

Would now be a good time to change?

How to Change Your Beliefs

The first step in changing a belief is to understand that it is just a thought that you keep repeating until you believe it to be true. It is not a proven fact.

Just acknowledging your belief as a mere thought will change your thinking because you accepted the fact that there might be an opposite to it. You know you can look into this to see whether your thought is the best one to help you achieve your desired results.

Let's look at a simple process that will help you change your limiting beliefs into empowering beliefs. Below is a template for you to use.

Your current, limiting belief	Your actions	The result
New empowering belief	**Actions that will get you to your new result**	**The new results that you would like to get**

There are two ways to go about this process. Either enter one of your limiting beliefs in box #1 then go through the process in the following order.

Your current, limiting belief	Your actions	The result
1	2	3
New empowering belief.	**Actions that will get you to your new result.**	**The new results that you would like to get.**
6	5	4

Alternatively, you can enter a result that you would like to change and try to figure out what's the limiting belief behind it. This means working backwards. Follow our numbers:

Your current limiting belief	Your actions	The result.
3	2	1
New empowering belief.	Actions that will get you to your new result.	The new results that you would like to get.
6	5	4

Let's use our example from above to see this process in action.

Your current, limiting belief	Your actions	The result
My employees are a liability to my company. I wish I could manage without them, and save the money I spend on their wages.	Not involving them in important decisions. Not encouraging them to share ideas. Paying them based on time and effort and not on results.	Sales are down and the future does not look too promising.

New empowering belief	Actions that will get you to your new result	The new results that you would like to get
Every employee is an asset to my company. My job is to help them develop their unique skills and abilities to create greater value for the company and the marketplace.	Get their input on all decisions. Encourage them to share ideas. Compensate them based on results.	A growing company with a great vision.

Your next step is to find a list of actions that you can do every day for the next 21 days, which will reinforce the new belief and make it part of your natural thinking process.

For example, you could schedule a meeting with your employees and ask them for suggestions that could impact the future of the company. You could also set a time to review the payroll and see how you can include some form of performance-based compensation.

Another great exercise you can use to enforce a new belief is to find evidence that supports the new belief. Using our example, you would look for evidence that supports the belief of "Every employee is an asset to the company, and my job is to help them develop their unique skills and abilities to create greater value for the company and the marketplace."

You will find plenty facts and stories to support your new belief, just as you have done to support your old, limiting belief. There

"If you can imagine it, you can achieve it; if you can dream it, you can become it."

William Arthur

is evidence all around us, and we just have to decide what we want to zoom in on. As soon as you decide – you will find it. Your mind works like a camera, allowing you to focus in on any area that you'd like to. Be careful where you zoom in, because that is what your mind will capture and remember forever.

Your Favorite Beliefs

Look at the vision you desire for your business and your life. Find the beliefs that will support that vision. Then build those beliefs up.

Why not spend the next 12 months working on changing one belief per month? If you do, you will have changed one major limiting belief for each of the top ten roles you play in life. The impact will change your results and your life in general.

Changing any belief will have a ripple effect across other areas additional your life. Every thought we have is a combination of all our beliefs combined, and changing one of them will change the thoughts and results for all of them.

Do you believe you can do it?

POINTS TO REMEMBER!

- Change your beliefs and your life will change.
- A belief is just a belief and you can change it any time you like.
- You are great, and you keep working every day to grow in all different roles you have in life.
- It's easier to succeed than to fail.

Chapter 5

WHAT DO YOU DO?

Why Knowing What You Do Is So Important

The first step in creating a successful business enterprise is to develop what's knows as a 'Unique Selling Proposition.' Rosser Reeves of Ted Bates & Company coined the term in the 1940s to differentiate between his products and those of his competition. Marketing experts and company executives has used it ever since. The Unique Selling Proposition (or USP) is the key ingredient of what makes your product, service, business or company "unique." It's what's special about your brand and what will turn your product from a commodity into something that consumers connect with and will refer others to with confidence.

Let's look at a famous brand as an example to better understand the importance of having a unique selling proposition. In 1917, Barnes & Noble opened its first store in New York City. If you had asked William Barnes and Clifford Noble at that time, "What do you do?" they would confidently had answered, "We sell books."

There was no need for anyone to define the uniqueness of their brand because, at that point in time, simply stating that your company "sold books" was all that the consumer needed to know.

Even in 1980, when Barnes & Noble already had 797 stores, the answer clearly remained, "We sell books." Most American consumers associated book shopping with Barnes & Noble.

But after a while they realized that selling books just isn't enough of a USP to survive in the long run, and they started the process of changing their USP based on the needs of the marketplace, constantly making changes to their business model to refocus on their brand and USP.

They've tried a lot of different things: Adding Starbucks as a co-retailer in their stores since 1993; the addition of music sections in-store; the addition of kids departments selling educational toys; building up their website and designing the NOOK. They knew that "we sell books" was no longer a defining USP.

The current CEO of Barnes and Noble may, today, answer the question of what Barnes & Noble does with:

- We sell 30 million items on our website including many books
- We have great shopping locations where you can spend family time with your kids
- We have the best wireless devices to enable you to read on the go
- We have an online marketplace where over 10,000 retailers sell their products

But if you want a simple, clear and definitive answer as to what Barnes and Noble now does, you won't get one. That's because they have to keep changing it as they go. Selling books alone can't be their focus anymore. Why? Because the market-place has evolved in the following ways:

a) Consumers are reading digital books vs. hard copies more than ever before

b) The online bookselling market has taken away B & N's ability to compete. Amazon keeps figuring out better distribution methods and are so able to sell at lower prices than other retailers

c) The publishing industry as a whole is undergoing sweeping changes due to the Internet

d) In recessionary times, discretionary spending is much tighter

Barnes and Noble did a great job by realizing early on that their future would be a digital one; their stores wouldn't survive selling hard copy books in a digital age. So they hired top executives from major digital players, and shifted their focus in that direction. In 2012 they expect to generate $1.8 billion from their Nook Line, which is showcased in their stores.

If they survive in the long run remains to be seen, but they certainly serve as a great example of a company that adapts their business to the changing times, adjusting their uniqueness to what their customers wanted to see

On the other hand, Borders bookstore wasn't able to adopt their USP to the changes in the marketplace, they opened their first location in 1971 and had 1291 stores by 2003. Although they also 'sold books', that was not enough. Borders wasn't able to make a profit selling books; their last profitable year was 2006. They filed for bankruptcy in February 2011 closing all of their stores.

When Microsoft founder Bill Gates was asked what he regretted, he said that in the middle of the 1990's, Microsoft knew that the Internet would start playing a big role in how people used their software and operating systems. Since this concern wasn't the highest on Microsoft's list, however, they didn't put many resources on it. By the time the Internet had made it into most homes becoming a household item, Microsoft was behind in the game. The door was opened to competition, and Microsoft never caught up as the frontrunner in cloud software sharing. Gates regrets that his company didn't realize how fast and strongly the Internet would grow, and that they weren't poised for meeting that demand.

The Power of a Brand

Which company can save you money on your car insurance? How do you spell 'cars for kids'?

If you answered 'Geico' to the first question and 'Kars for Kids' to the second question, you are aware of the power of a brand! Notice that neither answer is correct: Most drivers find that All State insurance will save them more money than Geico, and cars is definitely not spelled with a k.

Both Geico and Kars for Kids have succeeded in developing memorable brands. When a potential consumer thinks about solving the "saving money on car insurance" need or about getting rid of the old clunker in the garage, these are the brands that are top of mind.

I use these two companies as an example to stress the point that creating uniqueness works even if it's only in the name of the company or in their commercial messages. Most people don't have the time to research every claim made by a brand, so even if the claims are not entirely true, customers will likely go with the brand that comes to mind first.

Developing a brand has three components to it:

1) Creating the outline of the brand, what will be unique about it, and how will it execute or deliver that uniqueness

2) Finding a way to communicate the uniqueness of the brand to the public and tell them what it will do for them. Meaning, what need will it meet or problem will it solve

3) Ensuring that the brand delivers on its promise and gives people what they expect. This will build product loyalty and will generate word-of-mouth referrals, which will keep the brand growing

Most companies are not doing any one of these three activities! They haven't determined their unique selling proposition; they haven't written a plan of action for the brand's operation; they are not communicating with the public in specific and effective ways. They don't know their uniqueness, and they certainly are not delivering on their promise because they haven't made one!

Of course, some companies have taken one or two of these three key steps. Many have figured out their brand's uniqueness. But they need to communicate this to the public. If they don't, the public remains unaware of the brand, and the promise (that USP) is not delivered upon. The brand will so die.

Taking all three of these key brand actions takes dedication, vision and leadership. But it can be done! And it needs to be done in your company if you want it to succeed and create something that would stay around for decades.

Myths About Building a Brand

Let's look at some of the limiting beliefs that people have when it comes to building their brand.

PEOPLE KNOW WHAT I DO!

When I ask business owners to clarify what they do, they sometimes tell me that there is no reason to worry about it, since their customers know what they do.

The answer for you lies in considering this. If you were to ask 100 of your customers what it is that you do, would they offer a clear, specific answer, or would they offer a general answer such as what industry you are in?

For example, if you sell jewelry online, would 100 of your surveyed customers say that:

- You are in the jewelry business
- You sell jewelry online
- You are the best priced online jeweler
- You are the most knowledgeable online jewelry seller
- You are the online jewelry seller with the biggest selection

The first two answers are so general that they suggest that you are not much different than anyone else in your industry, or perhaps that you never took the initiative to build your company in a way to make your USP clear.

THERE IS NOTHING UNIQUE ABOUT MY PRODUCT OR SERVICE

I am still shocked every time someone answers me, "We are not any different than our competitors." I just don't see how they expect to be successful! In today's world, where there is so much competition for clients' attention and so many big players in the market, how does someone expect to compete if they can't identify at least one unique factor that distinguishes their business from the next? It's critical to create a focus for your company that makes it uniquely stand out from the crowd.

No matter what business you are in, there are always unmet needs which you can use to create a uniqueness for your business and stand out from the crowd.

I DON'T HAVE THE BUDGET TO BUILD A BRAND

I find that a lot of business people feel that building a brand requires a lot of money and so is only for large corporations with deep pockets. In my experience, this is not true: You can build a brand with no money at all.

Branding is not about having large billboard ads on major highways or having a television commercial on the Halftime at the Super Bowl. A brand doesn't even have to be a company selling nationwide; you can be a local pizza store and have a great brand without any advertisement at all.

The definition of a brand is that you create a strong reason why people should come to your store or buy your product. If you make the best pizza in town, people will walk past other pizza stores to get to yours because they want only your pizza. They may also want the experience of being at your store specifically. You can do this by creating a better product or experience without spending money on pricey advertising.

Companies spend millions of dollars in marketing to cover up the fact that they don't have a straightforward uniqueness. They think that as long as they spend enough money in marketing they will grow and succeed, but this is seldom the case. Marketing money is only justified if you can bring in a customer and keep him coming back to your company. That only happens when you have a uniqueness that they can get attached to. That way people get attached to your business, product or service when they visit for the first time and keep coming back to get that again.

You don't need a budget to build a brand. You need a clear vision and persistence in your actions. The results will follow.

Your Tagline

You will sometimes see a company that has clearly figured out what they do, and have created a powerful and memorable tagline that states it. When the message is clear, people will remember it and connect to it, and it will be easy for that company to build a loyal client base.

FEDEX CORPORATION: WHEN IT ABSOLUTELY, POSITIVELY HAS TO BE THERE OVERNIGHT.

FedEx was built on the promise of delivery on time since UPS was not good at doing so at that time. FedEx's message was very clear. It was not so much about them delivering packages, but about guaranteeing you on-time delivery. This offered the clients piece of mind, and this message was responsible for their unbelievable success.

DOMINO'S PIZZA: YOU GET FRESH, HOT PIZZA DELIVERED TO YOUR DOOR IN 30 MINUTES OR LESS OR IT'S FREE.

Two brothers with $500 and a clear tagline founded Domino's in 1960. They successfully built a billion-dollar empire around this simple promise. People want their pizza fast, and they knew where to get it, guaranteed.

STARBUCKS: NO TAGLINE

Starbucks never had a tagline, but they still managed to create a wildly popular brand of coffee shops that sell both coffee as well as the **experience** of coffee. Their name became synonymous with a great social status and experience that you get while enjoying a Starbucks latte.

SELLING STOCKS OR CREATING FINANCIAL INDEPENDENCE?

I n 2000, after the stock market crash with billions of dollars lost in overvalued Internet stocks, Merrill Lynch hired me to help their sales team get their confidence back. They needed to get back to calling potential clients but had lost the heart to do so. This was a big challenge, as they were coming off a 10-year bull run where investing in stocks was very popular. Investors made millions watching their stocks double every few months, and the Merrill Lynch sales team had an easy time convincing people to keep investing during that run.

But that changed in March of 2000 when a chain of events started a market fear that Internet stocks would not be able to keep growing as expected. From early March to early April of 2000, the NASDAQ fell from 5048 points to 3649, creating fear and insecurity like never before in the history of the stock market.

Imagine being a stock seller then: In order to make a living you had to convince people that the best thing they could do was to invest in stocks! It didn't make sense, but the sales people at Merrill lynch had to get new accounts to keep their salary and commissions going.

After talking with their top sales people in New York, it was clear to me that they saw themselves as sales people selling stocks. If we were going to get them back to confident selling, we would have to change their USP as well as their beliefs about what they were doing.

Although it was true that they were selling stocks, there were many other ways to look at it. The first thing that we looked at was why people buy stocks. We wondered if it was because they loved to own those stocks or because they were looking for the potential growth and financial security that stocks offered.

We had the sales team answer the following questions:

- *Do you feel that people should own stocks in their portfolio?*
- *What percentage of a personal portfolio should be stocks vs. other, more secure investments?*
- *Do people need to build their investment portfolio? Why?*

- *How can you help them?*
- *What do you do?*

  If we had given the Merrill Lynch sales team these questions in 1999 their answers would have been:
- *Do you feel that people should own stocks in the portfolio? Yes*
- *What percentage of people portfolio should be stocks? 90%*
- *Do people need to build their investment portfolio? Why? Yes, you can make money fast...*
- *How can you help them? I can show them which stocks are hot now.*
- *What do you do? I sell stocks*

  But in 2000, after the Crash, their answers were:
- *Do you feel that people should own stocks in the portfolio? Yes*
- *What percentage of people portfolio should be stocks vs. other more secure investments? 10-20%*
- *Do people need to build their investment portfolio? Why? Yes! People have to build a strong financial foundation that would work for them no matter how the stock market does.*
- *How can you help them? By working with them to understand their needs and create a balanced portfolio that would be 80% secured investment and 20% stocks to create the perfect balance between security and growth.*
- *What do you do? I am working with people to help them achieve their financial goals.*

  The difference was amazing. When a team who saw themselves as sellers of stocks had to call prospective people, they felt rejected before even picking up the phone, all because they knew that nobody would be interested in investing in stocks after the stock market crashed!

On the other hand, when they saw themselves as workers in helping people achieve financial growth, they knew that most people would need and use that service. After that, it was about building clients trust in the company, their message and their products.

With this approach, the fact that the market had crashed and people were afraid of investing in stocks actually worked to the sales team's advantage. Now the sales reps wanted the same thing as their potential clients, which was to build a strong and balanced portfolio that will survive downturns in the market. And this team knew that they had the knowledge and expertise to help clients accomplish this.

With most of these sales people, the approach worked wonders. They went back to the phones excited about the new opportunities they saw. But, we all have a choice as to what we believe: Other sales people didn't allow this approach to work – they insisted on keeping their old beliefs and victim status.

How to Find Your Uniqueness

In every industry you can find a unique niche to fill, which will give you an opportunity to build a loyal following and a successful business. In order for your unique selling proposition to work, it needs to be a combination of the following two factors:

1) It works well with who you are. Something that will align well with your unique combination of passion and skills.

2) It makes good business sense; you are filling a need that the marketplace will appreciate and will pay for.

Sometimes we have a need in our business and have no way to fill it. If so, chances are good that other business owners have this too, which gives us an opportunity to focus on filling this need and creating a USP.

To generate ideas on the right USP, consider speaking with 20 of your customers to ask them what they like and don't like about your business or industry. You may need to ask specific questions in order to get detailed answers.

For example, you might ask:

- What one thing would you like to see improved in our industry?

- When and why do you get frustrated when using our product, or service?

- If you had to open a business in this industry what would you do differently?

If you find that you are getting similar answers from multiple customers, you may have discovered a real need that's unmet in your industry. If you can find a way to fill that need, you might discover a unique selling proposition that will allow you to stand out in the marketplace.

STRUCTURAL CHANGE BASED ON CUSTOMER-EXPRESSED NEED

While working with Marc Tash interiors (www. marctashinteriors.com), a large home interior design company in NYC, the main focus of the *company was reupholstering furniture and providing window treatments. But when we surveyed their customers, we heard about popular interest in having other parts of the house redesigned at the same time as well.*

When people decide to give their home a facelift, they want to consider the big picture and see what they could do to upgrade the look and feel of the entire house. They wanted an expert designer to come in and advise them on which parts of the house to upgrade. While upholstery and window treatments were definitely part of this, many people felt that they needed more.

By Marc Tash not offering that service, they lost business from potential customers who went looking for another interior designer to advise them. In doing this, the customers had to pay for the advice and also deal with the contractors who executed the designer's plans.

Marc Tash saw the results of this survey and decided to create a unique service: They would offer free, full house interior design consultation and take full responsibility of executing their plan (once approved by the client) together with the necessary contractors, so that the client would never have to deal with them directly. This saved the client money, effort and potential hassle, and made Marc Tash stand out from his peers.

Standing Out

Let's look at some of the common ways of standing out from the crowd. Notice that most of the options fall on the extremes of the business spectrum, because to stand out and be noticeable from among the crowd you want to be extreme on one end of what's possible. In most cases there will be a crowd that would like your extreme uniqueness, and its members will become loyal fans.

BIGGEST SELECTION:

A giant selection gives consumers confidence that you are not pushing them to buy only the items that you have, but the items that they need, since you have everything available. People also feel good about looking around and making their choice based on the selection available. Could you find a niche where you would have the biggest selection of products or services available?

LIMITED EDITIONS:

Many successful businesses have been built on this concept – from clothing to jewelry to alcoholic beverages. The fact that something is 'limited' makes it special and unique, and people who want to belong to that "exclusive group" are always on the lookout for rare products that are not available to the general public. Is there somewhere in your industry that you can create a unique line that is limited and so not available to everyone?

SPEED:

We already touched on the examples of Dominos Pizza and FedEx: companies who built their success on speed of delivery. Making a promise on speed is a big commitment that requires an efficient system to be in place. In most cases, however, it is well worth it, because there is always a group of consumers who will pay more because they need a product or service faster than the current system can offer.

Especially with online sellers, I have seen that the use of a guarantee that all orders will ship same day has increased sales over 20%. Even when the people ordering don't know how long it will take to get delivery, the fact that you are shipping right away gives many the confidence that they will get it faster than if they shop with your competition.

Achieving 'uniqueness' is hard act to teach. In fact, teaching something inherently means that the thing is no longer unique. What makes something unique is the fact that it is fresh and new and fills a need in a novel way.

What makes your favorite store/brand your favorite? Although their particular uniqueness might not be right for your industry, the more you investigate just what it is that makes your favorite companies so special, the more your mind will try to configure your own uniqueness.

What's Your Story?

Sometimes the best way to create your uniqueness is to double back to your origins. How did you get started in your business or company? In some cases there is a passionate story behind getting into the business that can help you create and build its brand.

One of the most powerful ways of building a brand is to share your story with the public. Share the passion that you have for your company and the vision that you created for its future, and customers will warm up to this passion and turn to loyal supporters.

Since we are so bombarded with information, messages and sales pitches all day long, most people are looking to connect with the things they chose to buy. Most of us are looking for a connection that will give us more than just the item that we need – we want to feel part of something that we admire and support.

When I first read the book, "Pour Your Heart into It: How Starbucks Built a Company One Cup at a Time" by Howard Schultz, I was pulled into the passion and emotion that was behind that cup of coffee. After feeling this emotion, I no longer looked at the product as simply a cup of coffee. I now looked at it as a brand, as a story that I could connect to. Now that's a lot more than just brewed beans!

Every time I sit down with a new client, I ask, "How did you get started in this business?" Most of the time, I can see them recall an old memory as they start telling me the story behind their business. This is when I see them get back to the original passion and energy they had when they started out.

Often, their story is a very moving one with much emotion attached to it. Sometimes there will be a very unique reason why the client went into business. This specific and unique reason usually gets lost over time and the company often falls in line with what everyone else is doing instead of continuing to distinguish themselves.

How to Resurrect Your Focus

In the following pages is a step-by-step process that you can use to identify your uniqueness in your field and build your brand on it so that you stand out from the crowd.

FIND YOUR USP

What do you do? _____
_____
_____

What are the 3 biggest issues that you think your clients would like to see changed in the industry?

1) _____
_____
_____

2) _____
_____
_____

3) _____
_____
_____

Call 10 of your clients and ask them what they like about doing business with you. Ask what would they like to see changed or improved.

1) _____
_____
_____

2) _____
_____
_____

3) _____
_____
_____

4) _____

_____

_____

5) _____

_____

_____

6) _____

_____

_____

7) _____

_____

_____

8) _____

_____

_____

9) _____

_____

_____

10) _____

_____

_____

Using all the answers to the above, select the two issues or needs that you feel most people can relate to:

1) _____

_____

_____

2) _____
_____
_____

Can you think of any other industry that has similar issues to the one you're in?

_____
_____

If yes, how do they solve this issue?

_____
_____
_____

Could you think of a similar approach that might work in your industry?

_____
_____
_____

List three businesses that you admire or enjoy dealing with.

_____
_____
_____
_____

Describe a specific thing they do that has left an impression on you.

_____
_____
_____

What can you change in your business to elicit a similar feeling from your customers?

_____

_____

_____

_____

_____

Let's look at how we used this form to make changes at a local shoe store.

What do you do?

I sell children's shoes

What are the 3 biggest issues that you think your clients would like to see changed in the industry?

1) *There are long waiting lines during season.*

2) *Prices are too high for most families in the area.*

3) *There are not enough choices.*

Call 10 of your clients and ask them what they would like to see changed or improved?

1) *Faster service during season.*

2)*Better quality shoes at more affordable pricing.*

3) *More hours after school.*

4) *Find a way the get people in and out more quickly during the busy season.*

5) *Eliminate long lines.*

6) *Open later hours at night.*

7) *Sell at better prices.*

8) *The wait time during season is crazy.*

9) *Better prices.*

10) *Longer night hours.*

Pick the 2 issues/needs that you feel the most people can relate to:

1) *The wait time during season/night hours.*

2) *Better pricing.*

Can you think of any other industry that has similar issues to the one that you just wrote down?

The clothing industry – where people can't afford the sticker prices. Also, doctor's offices often have long lines.

If yes, then how do they solve this issue?

- *They offer an additional line of lower priced clothing, for those looking to pay less.*
- *Some doctors' offices will see people by appointment only, which eliminates the waiting time.*

Could you think of a similar approach that might work in your industry?

- *We could bring in a new line of lower priced shoes.*
- *We could designate a few hours a day where we close to the public and give families appointments to buy shoes for the entire family.*
- *And we can also find a way to stay open later at night.*

Write down three businesses that you admire or enjoy dealing with, and what specifically do you like about them?

The Apple store – *The comfortable store environment and helpful staff.*

My local dry goods store – *The fact that they remember the details about my family and always ask me how they are doing.*

Wal-Mart – *Hugh selection and always open.*

What can you change in your business to garner similar liking from your customers?

- *Create a comfortable environment.*
- *Remember to take notes about clients' families.*
- *Have a bigger selection and be open longer hours than anyone else in the industry.*

Now we have a general list of specific things that we can do, which will create uniqueness for the store and help build and shape a brand.

- Bring in a lower priced brand.
- Offer appointments for larger families during season time.
- Stay open later hours at night.
- Create a comfortable environment in the store.
- Remember your clients and their families.

POINTS TO REMEMBER!

- Create a unique selling proposition.
- Make sure it's unique and in demand in today's market place.
- You don't need money to build a brand; you need a clear compelling message.
- Share your story with the marketplace.

Chapter 6

HOW TO DO IT

Creating and implementing processes.

Now that you have figured out the best answer to the question of what you do, it's time to move on to the next step, which is HOW you do it. It is time to take a closer look at the processes you have in place: from how your product or service is handled, to the first interaction between a customer and your company, and all the way through this ongoing relationship.

Creating clear processes for every aspect of your business will give you the opportunity to deliver your USP to the marketplace smoothly, solidly and consistently, and that's what builds brand loyalty.

You've worked hard on identifying and developing your unique selling proposition, but, without all the necessary processes in place, your company won't be able to deliver it. Your customers won't return and won't refer their friends to you. You must set up the experience you want for your brand and deliver it every time. Your customers not only want it – they expect it.

As a business owner, you can walk me through your business and explain to me all the activity that's being done on daily bases. You can show me how business comes in, how it's being delivered and how customer service does its problem-solving. But this is not enough, as long as you don't turn it into a predictable process where you will know what's going to happen and when the results will come to be. And if you don't like the results you should know which parts of the process have to change.

Let's use Wal-Mart as an example. This American success story now has 8,500 stores in 15 countries, and billions of dollars in annual sales. There is a great deal to be learned from this. But first, what do you think their most important success ingredient is?

They don't have the lowest prices on the market and they don't have the biggest selection of inventory in their stores. But they do have processes. In fact, Wal-Mart has thousands of process in place: from how to open a new store, to how inventory is controlled and managed and beyond. Every process they use has been analyzed and implemented, and it continues to be assessed and modified. The combined effect of all their processes is the key to the success of their empire.

Wal-Mart is one of the largest trucking companies in the world. Trucking? Yes, every night they move inventory from store to store in order to adjust their inventory levels in each one. This ensures that each location has what they need based on their weather forecast for the next day and on their customer base and so on.

This might seem like a simple task but it isn't. When you look at any retail business you will find that one of the biggest challenges is the ability to manage inventory. This key task requires a lot of processes to be in place, and to be continually measured and modified to ensure successful results. Whether it's Wal-Mart, McDonalds, Amazon or any large successful corporation, you can be sure that they all have solid processes firmly in place for every part of their business.

What is a Process?

A business process collects related and relevant tasks or activities and combines them into a set way of doing things in order to produce a product, service or goal. A process can be as simple as the company policy as to how to answer the phone or send out the business mail; or it can be as complex as a flowchart of actions that branch out into a variety of sequences to be followed.

I recently visited an office and saw lots of outgoing mail piled up at the reception desk. When I asked the receptionist why that mail hasn't been sent out, she explained that they had run out of the rolls that fill the stamp printer. They would have to wait 5-7 business days for the new rolls to arrive. In the meantime the mail piled up and the staff, unaware of this complication, was telling customers that their checks were 'in the mail.'

I asked the receptionist about the process in place for the ordering of these rolls; she explained that there was no need for a process since each order of rolls lasts for at least 6 months, and they know already when to reorder.

Based on this, I asked her why then they hadn't put the order in a few weeks before, when the supply was low. She didn't know the answer. When I asked the office manager who was responsible for reordering the rolls, he replied that anyone in the office could order them, but no one was responsible.

My advice was to create a process for this: Put someone in charge of checking the supplies once a month and make the ordering far enough in advance to ensure that this didn't happen again.

This may seem like a very minor and insignificant example, - and it is - but it did lead to a delay in the business mail for a week. It looked very bad for the business and aggravated the customers. All those problems – from one minor supply glitch. How many other little glitches happen in your company, and how much trouble does this add up to, over the course of a year? It can all be avoided with processes in place.

Prevent It or Deal With It

A process can drive the doing something right from the beginning in order to prevent issues from happening. But it can also be put into place to deal with issues when they arise. In business, as in life, things do happen no matter how much you try to get it all right from the start.

One of my customers recently had his secretary send a package to their accountant. It was full of important tax documents and UPS lost it. They apologized and sent a refund of $36 for the lost documents. Unfortunately, the secretary didn't copy the documents before sending them. Now she has to spend many hours over the course of many weeks to get copies of the documents from various vendors. Some of them may never be recovered.

The boss had told his secretary, when he hired her, that any important documents needed to be copied and scanned before they left the office. However, this procedure was never implemented into a process that she had to follow. It was never written down, and there was nothing put in place to ensure that this process was adhered to.

Let The Process Work For You

One of the greatest challenges in business is that you are busy with so many little details, like delivering the product or service, running from one emergency to the next, managing the daily activity of the business. At the end of the day, there's no time left to grow the business.

One of the main benefits of creating processes in your business is that once a process is implemented you don't have to worry about whether and how it's being done. You know that the process is in place and will be implemented, which allows you the freedom of focusing on other parts of the business.

To be successful, you have to work **on** your business – not just **in** your business. Your job is to create the system that will deliver your vision to the world. Once your vision is clear, you want to create the processes that will carry it out. You can then outsource or hire people to follow your process. You can also focus on improving or expanding the processes that you have created or build something new.

It's Predictable!

Having a process is the only way to create predictable results. This will assure you that the customer will get what he was promised and will make him confident that he will get this each and every time he does business with you. This, as we said earlier, leads to the almighty word-of-mouth.

People love certainty. Many people love to shop in malls because they know what to expect there. Many people, for the same reason, fear dealing with smaller stores (or brands) because they are unsure of how they will be treated and of what inventory they will find. The more processes you have in place, the more certainty you offer to your customers. This includes customer service, product pricing, your return policy, etc.

It Could Be Improved!

Nothing is perfect and everything can be improved. There are times in business when we know that we have to change the way we do things. Maybe we are getting negative feedback from our customers, or we realize that our current way of doing something is not the most cost-effective way, and we could somehow do it better.

Let's look at a simple example. One of your employees has an unusual way of answering his phone. One day a customer complains that this employee doesn't answer the phone in a professional manner. Let's say you thank him for the feedback, find this employee and tell them to be more professional when picking up the phone. The employee agrees to do this and you move on to keep up with your busy day. A week later, you get another complaint about the same issue. You may be frustrated but you didn't properly implement a change in process.

If you would've created and written up a process for how phone calls should be answered, you would have solved the problem (or, if not, you would have revamped this process.) Dealing with a process is much better than dealing with complaints.

Processes Keep The Brand Consistent.

How do you train your new employees? Most businesses have no official training policy; the new employee gets trained on the job either by you or another employee who shows them what to do and how.

If any of your key employees leaves the company without notice or has a personal emergency that takes them away suddenly, how difficult will it be to train a new hire to replace that employee? How many mistakes will a new hire make before learning the right way of doing things? Can you afford someone to learn on your existing customer base? Do you have the time to monitor how a new employee communicates with customers and represents your brand? No, you don't!

This is why the processes that you develop and implement must be written down. Once a clear process is in place for every series of tasks in each department, all you need to do is hand over the written process to the new and/ or existing employee. This will spell it all out for them and you can hold them accountable to follow the exact steps of the process. Since it is in writing, it can easily be reviewed at any time.

Each Department Needs Its Processes.

Most organizations have the following four departments:

Sales – how new business comes in.

Marketing – how you promote or communicate your product of services.

Operations – how you manufacture or deliver your product or service.

Finance – pricing of goods, income & expenses.

Each one of these departments requires many processes to be set up and executed.

Let's look at some of the basic tasks that need a process developed and implemented to ensure your success.

SALES

Everything starts with a sale, and there are a lot of ways to get them: hiring full-time sales people, using strategic relationships, etc. No matter what your sales channels are, they need to be systemized by the use of processes so that they are predictable and measurable.

If you have sales people, you want a process for finding them, training them, compensating them, etc.

If you are getting sales from strategic relationships that you have built, you want to have a process for how you find these relationships, how you maintain them, etc.

If you have an in-house sales team, you want to have a process for finding the right people, for training them, compensating them, etc.

MARKETING

What process is in place for marketing your company? How do you decide on your marketing budget? How do you choose which marketing channels to use? How do you measure the success of your marketing campaigns? Processes will help turn all those unanswered questions into a clearly predictable brand.

OPERATIONS

If you are manufacturing a product, you need process for finding the right vendors, for buying and maintaining your equipment, for hiring and training your employees, for quality control and for measuring productivity, etc.

If you are a retail store, you need processes for purchasing, pricing, for customer service, for processing transactions, for handling complaints and returns, etc.

If you are a services business, you need processes for how to deliver the service from initial contact with a customer straight through to the delivery of that service.

FINANCE

There are lots of processes when it comes to finance – depending on the type of business you are in. In general, you need to have a process for running various reports each month, a process to ensure that you are buying at the best possible prices, a process to constantly check if your products or services are priced competitively, etc.

How To Set Up Processes

Since most business owners are not analytical and don't get excited about setting up detailed processes and systems, let us help. Below is a basic step-by-step guide on how to get your business from zero written systems to a well-oiled company with all necessary processes in place.

STEP 1

Take out four pieces of paper (or open four documents on the computer.) Title each of these with a separate department: sales, marketing, operations and finance. Add more if you have more specific departments in place.

STEP 2

Write down any and all tasks that are being done in that department; it doesn't matter how big or small, or how often the task is done.

For example, the tasks for an operations department might be:

- Order office supplies
- Open alarm system and doors in the morning
- Check inventory
- Place reorder
- Print order slips
- Print UPS labels
- Package orders
- Close office at night
- Etc.

STEP 3

Once you have a basic list of tasks for each department, review the list to make sure you didn't leave anything out. Sometimes we are so used to doing a task that we don't even identify it as one. Things like answering phones, checking emails and opening business mail may be done automatically and without much thought, but they need to show up on your list. Other things happen infrequently, such as preparing for a trade show that happens only once a year, but that too needs to get on your list.

To help you find these 'hidden' tasks, keep a memo pad handy for one full day. Write down every little thing that you do all day long, and then, at the end of the day, look at all those little things and identify the tasks.

Another neat way to find the hidden tasks is by looking through all your emails from the past two weeks; these will show the communication for a lot of tasks.

If you find yourself wondering, "Is this a task?" the answer is always yes. If you had to do it or if someone else had to do it on your behalf it is a task.

For example, if you found yourself looking at mail that you sent out but that was returned because the address was invalid, you have found a task that has to be done at your company: Verify all business addresses at some regular interval. Add it to your list.

STEP 4

At this point you should have all your four (or more) lists of tasks. Now it's time to break those tasks down into a detailed process. This means that if I had to step into your shoes today, I would simply follow the steps that take me through each task, and I would be able to do so without even knowing anything about your business.

Let's use ordering office supplies as an example:

Task: Ordering office supplies.

Frequency: Every second Tuesday.

Responsibility: Employee such-and-such.

1 - Print out the office supply list.

In order for this task to be done efficiently you would need another task: Write down every single item that is used in the office and create a comprehensive list of office supplies. The list will need to be updated every one, three or six months with any new items added. This list will also serve to identify how many units your company needs to have in stock at all times of each supply. This way you will never run out of them.

2 - Walk around the office and write down how much you have from each item.

3 - Create a new order list from all the items that have to be ordered.

4 – Phone, email or place the order on the supply company website.

5 - If an item is not in stock, go to..... And order it there.

6 - Have the order delivered to......

7 - Pay for the order with......

8 - Give/email receipt to......

You can do this in a lot more detail if you like, but I think a basic rundown of the steps is all you need to have a process in place.

The process of ordering office supplies is now completed, and you can move on to outline the next task on your list.

STEP 5

Take your document with the outline of the task, and give it to someone who has never done this task before. Ask them to follow the steps in the process and see if they can do this easily. This will tell you if any necessary steps were omitted. The process may be second nature to you or an employee, but for someone who has never done it before, it needs to be clear, concise and thorough or they will get stuck.

STEP 6

Buy four binders, one for each department, and place the relevant list of tasks in each. Add an index, and then put in each outlined task as you complete writing down their process.

STEP 7

Outline at least one process every day, until you have written down your entire task list for your company.

STEP 8

Review all processes every six months to make sure they are being followed. Update changes as needed, and always keep the process binders current with company and industry changes.

As we go through to next few chapters in the book, a lot of new ideas will pass through your mind. New processes that will strengthen your USP will leap out at you. When that happens, take out a blank piece of paper and write these new ideas down as tasks. Then you can fill in the details of how this task should be done, and hand it over to one of your staff member to execute.

> *"Virtually every company will be going out and empowering their workers with a certain set of tools, and the big difference in how much value is received from that will be how much the company steps back and really thinks through their business processes, thinking through how their business can change, how their project management, their customer feedback, their planning cycles can be quite different than they ever were before."*
>
> Bill Gates

POINTS TO REMEMBER!

- Most problems in your business are there because there are no processes in place
- Creating processes builds a brand
- Don't do it. Instead, create a process on how it should get done
- You have the vision for your business, but you might not be the best person to do the work

Chapter 7

THE RIGHT TEAM

Fire Half of Your Employees

What would happen if you fired half of your employees? In many of the companies that I've worked with, the answer is that not much would change! That is because the remaining employees would just fill in for and do the work of the fired employees.

Many companies are still stuck in the factory age. That was the age in which large factories had multitudes of employees working from 9am to 5pm, manufacturing a product on an assembly line. More employees in the corporation meant a bigger corporation, and that was a measure of success.

That has all changed with the death of the factory era and the start of the results economy. In today's world it's not the one that has the biggest employee count who wins, but whoever can deliver the best results for the biggest profit who wins. Those 2 are not related, since you can deliver the same results today without having any employees by outsourcing the work or by employing the right technology to get the work done.

One of the biggest challenges that companies are struggling with in recent years is the fact that they have a high overhead because of their employees – this shaves profits. They also have to compete with newcomers to their field who are somehow managing to deliver the same product or service at a lower price because they don't have the overhead, and that allows them to work at a lower profit margin.

With one third of the world already on the Internet, you can get almost anything done from your bedroom as you sit in your pajamas. You can have people give you product ideas, while other people can manufacture your idea into a product, have it delivered to a fulfillment center that will storage and ship your products, while a call center will sell your product and provide your customer service. You can do all of that without having to pay anyone a salary or benefits.

This has created a new playing field with more and more people moving into the freelance world, doing the work that they are passionate about and getting paid for results. This gives small businesses, as well as any large company, the opportunity to get work done

> *"The factory of the future will have only two employees, a man and a dog. The man will be there to feed the dog. The dog will be there to keep the man from touching the equipment."*
>
> Warren G. Bennis

without the overhead and cash flow that big companies usually need to keep their operations going. Another big change is that technology is replacing a lot of jobs that a few years ago required humans. This has caused any layoffs because companies can't afford to pay employees for tasks that their competitors have automated with technology.

You Need Team Members

There is a big difference between an employee and a team member. An employee will do whatever you tell them to do, as long as you tell them to do it. An employee can't take responsibility for a specific outcome as they are only focused on action. An employee may be afraid to take risks in doing something that might not work out and for which they will be blamed so they will stay in the zone that they think is secure.

If you look closely you will find that most tasks in your company require someone who can make their own decisions as long as they keep in mind the clear outcome that has to be achieved and use common sense to get there.

This is what team members do. They take the outcome that has to be accomplished and they work towards it, making decisions along the way, overcoming inevitable obstacles, asking for help when they need, and then reporting to you on the outcome of their project.

Some of your existing employees might be natural team leaders if given the chance. By helping them make the transition from employee to team member, you will find that their productivity will increase dramatically.

Passion VS Time

One of the main differences between an employee and a team member is that an employee will do anything you want them to do regardless of whether or not they have a passion for that particular thing. On the other hand, a team member who is responsible for generating a particular outcome in a specific area of the business will need to have a strong passion (as well as the relevant abilities) in order to succeed and deliver great results.

Human beings are all born with special talents and inborn skills. One of the old Jewish sages said that as God created each animal with its set of skills and talents to find its food, he did the same for humans, creating each one of us with our unique set of tools to make a living and provide for our families.

How do you know what your unique abilities are? Here are three signs that I learned from Dan Sullivan, the founder of Strategic Coach Inc. to identify your unique abilities:

YOU ENJOY DOING THEM FOR LONG PERIODS OF TIME

We all have tasks that we can do for hours and not realize how much time we have spent since we enjoy it so much. On the other hand, we all have tasks that make each minute drag on since those tasks don't come to us naturally and we have to push hard to get the task done.

THE MORE WE DO IT THE BETTER WE GET AT IT

When we use our natural ability, we get better at things the more we do them. If you really enjoy a certain sport, you will improve at it the more you do it. On the other hand, if you are playing a sport only because you have to, you might stay at the same level for years.

YOU WILL DELIVER GREAT RESULTS

If we do something that matches our unique ability, we will deliver better-than-average results, since we do it with a passion that introduces our natural creativity to the mix. This always results in a better product or service than if done by someone who does not have their passion in it.

To summarize: The ideal team in a business would be a group of people where each member is responsible to deliver in the areas of their unique ability. This means that the company, as a whole, will put out exceptional results in all areas.

The Ideal Company Structure

The most logical way to succeed is to have a team of people to whom you delegate a desired outcome and have them do whatever it takes to reach that result. To succeed in any business today, you have to do very well in very many areas, and you can't do that on your own. There is not enough time in the day to do all that has to be done, and you may not always be the best person for every single task.

You want to find people who have a natural talent in the area that you need help with, and outsource that part of the business to them. You will need to give them clear instructions of what your desired outcome is, give them whatever tools they need to achieve this goal, and then hold them accountable to achieve results.

Imagine having a team of four leaders in your company, each one of them assuming full responsibility for their department. The one in charge of sales works all day long to improve the sales of the company. The one in charge of marketing focuses on all marketing issues from finding the best places to market your business to creating the metrics to measure the return on investment. The third team member takes full responsibility in the operations department, from finding the right systems to creating new systems and implementing them. The fourth team member is in charge of all enterprise finances, creating reports that measure all aspects of profit and loss.

All four team members report to you weekly, giving you a clear picture of what's working and what needs improvement. All of them work together to create changes that will make the company more efficient and more profitable, and all of them do this at the same time while allowing you to focus on the overall picture and input your guidance where needed.

Why Don't You Have Team Members?

I find that most businesses have too many employees and too few team members. This may be because things were never organized into systems and processes to begin with. Such initial imbalances create one big mess with nonstop "urgent matters" cropping up one after another.

The owners of these businesses, not knowing what to do, keep adding employees to the system, thinking that the more people they have the more things will get done. They hire more and wait for the day when things are organized and quiet, so that they can focus on the long-term goals of the company.

But that day never comes, since adding people is not the solution. It only creates more situations for things to go wrong since more people are involved in each task. Creating systems is the right solution because it will eliminate most of the problems before they have a chance to happen.

I have seen two identical businesses with similar amounts of sales and customers. One business had one employee and the other business had six employees. The company with only one employee had a smoother operation going on than did the other.

The reason is that the first company had an owner who created systems on how things should be done. He hired an employee to work systematically. He continually monitored and adjusted his systems to keep things running smoothly.

The company with six employees never created systems. Each employee did everything and no one took responsibility for anything. Every one of the six employees did things the way they felt like doing it, causing confusion and frustration. Every new employee just added to the confusion and frustration by doing things their own way.

> "Lack of proper prior planning on your part does not constitute an emergency on mine."
>
> Old English Proverb

Don't Do It!

You might be the best person to create the vision for your company. You know how it should operate and how your customers should be treated. But you may also be the worst person to actually plan it all out!

Sometimes we tend to mix things up, and believe that since we are the ones who developed the vision, we are the ones who need to carry it out. But that may not always be the case. You can't be an entrepreneur and at the same time be a great sales person, a marketing expert, an operations manager, and a bookkeeper, etc.

Most entrepreneurs are by nature great thinkers. They can visualize the potential of an idea. They can persuade others to see things the way they themselves do. They know how close deals. But, in most cases, they don't have the critical attention to detail needed to run operations or finance.

So, the secret to success is to find the right person for the job and delegate that job to him. Then, through reviewing the reports they prepare for you, you can maintain enough control over each area of your business.

How to Transform Your Employees Into Team Members

In order to be a successful team member, a person has to feel confident that their talents and skills will achieve the desired outcome. They also need the confidence to make their own decisions even if they will turn out to be the wrong decisions.

Most people have the ability to be team members and achieve great results in their area of talent and passion. Unfortunately, over the years, they may be shoved and pushed down by others driving them to the point where they stop taking risks and give up on using their talents. They may act like robots and try to stay as safe as possible by doing only the things that pose little or no risk to them.

Your first step is to identify a talent that employees have and encourage them to focus on it in order to produce greater results for the company. It's possible that they are working in their area of expertise and natural talent, but it's also possible that you may need to switch them around to a different area to let their work match their passions.

Start by complimenting them on small things that you like about their work. The more you do this, the more confidence they will have in their own ability to take risks and produce great results.

Your next step is to start asking them for advice. Ask them how they would solve a certain situation that has come up in the business. This will accomplish two things: It will slowly train them to make decisions on their own by being involved in that process with you, and it will allow them to see that you trust their decision-making process and respect their way of thinking.

Every time they ask you for a decision, ask them what **they** think the right decision is. This shows them that you trust their common sense and expertise to make educated decisions. You might find that they are naturally making the best decisions for the business, and if they don't, you can share with them your way of thinking and how you would go about deciding. By doing that, you will give them the right tools to make decisions in the future.

Another important behavioral process is to teach employees that making mistakes is part of every successful project, and it's okay to make a mistake as long as you learn from it not to make the same mistake again. This is important because the fear of making a

"Trying to be secure is very risky."

Maurice Stein

mistake holds us back from doing what we are capable of doing, and there is no other way to grow and succeed but to make mistakes and learn from them.

There is no official process to transform someone from an employee to a team member. If you change your focus to discuss the desired outcomes with them – instead of just telling them what to do – and give them the confidence that they have what it takes to achieve those results, they will slowly change their focus as well.

Being Busy vs. Being Efficient

Realize that you are not making money when your employees are 'busy.' You are making money when they deliver results. Sometimes business owners are so worried that their employees have a few extra minutes during the day where they take care of personal business that they load them up with a lot of things to do just to make sure that they are always busy.

The challenge with this approach is that the employees start to think that the most important thing in the business is to be and look busy, regardless of what they are busy with or what results are generated.

It is a lot more efficient for your employees to know what results they are expected to achieve and to be in clear understanding of their responsibilities. Put your focus on helping them achieve those results regardless of whether they look busy or not. Give them the confidence to know that it's fine for them not to look busy – as long as you are both clear with what they contribute to the company.

Would you rather have busy employees, or team members who deliver you the results your company needs, even if they are left with two hours of free time every day?

Get Out of Their Way!

In order for you to have a successful team that will keep improving the different parts of your business, you have to learn how to delegate responsibility to them. They must clearly know your desired outcome, and from there on you can get out of their way. Leave them to do their work. You want them to use their passion in their own way and generate your target results. This won't happen unless you **let** them do it their way.

You can provide them with clear processes on how you want things done, but in most cases those processes have to be constantly improved based on industry changes. Since you can't write down every possible scenario, there are always some parts of every process that are left to the team members to decide on how to deal with.

Most of us like to be constantly involved with our employees, and we feel that we know how to do things better than anyone else. And so we check their work and tell them how we think it should all be done. The problem with this approach is that, without realizing it, we are converting them from team members into employees. If we continue on like this for a while, they will give up their creativity and start following what we are telling them to do. This means that they will not do anything on their own for fear of being criticized, and that is the opposite of why we hired them in the first place.

Over the years, I have seen this over and over. The owner will tell me to talk to his high-paid team members and find out why they can't get things done on their own. He feels that the company is losing money and that his employees are underperforming.

After talking to the staff, it is clear that they started with great intention to utilize their skills and take full responsibility in delivering the results that the company needed. However, as soon as they composed their first email (which the owner required he receive a copy of before it went out), the owner ran to the employee's office with advice on email writing.

After a few days, employees saw that they need to ask the boss before they do anything, if they want him to be happy with their performance. They feared he would get upset and blame them for performance hiccups if they don't ask him.

At the end of the day, some business owners will find themselves with high-salary team members who sit around waiting for the owner to tell them what to do. The owner doesn't have the time (and perhaps not the skill) to guide people in all areas. So their waiting around only costs the company in overhead without delivering the results that they were hired for, and it's nobody's fault.

Some employees spend a big portion of their time figuring out how to do things the way it would make their boss happy, instead of focusing on what's good for the business and its customers.

In the latter case, my first step would be for the employer to remove himself from receiving copies on all emails. This can feel scary in the beginning because it means letting go of control. But it allows me to then work with each team member in recreating their responsibilities, verifying the outcome they are being trusted with, and also working out how they will report their results.

In one case I sent the CEO on a three-month vacation! It turned out to be the best thing that ever happened to him and

> *"Never tell people how to do things. Tell them what to do and they will surprise you with their ingenuity."*
>
> General George Smith Patton, Jr.

his company. While on vacation, he came up with 6 new projects to propel his business into new markets. And Without his presence, the company had 3 months to organize all departments and have the team members take charge in their departments, setting goals and delivering results.

Lead and Coach!

Your focus as CEO should be to hire and develop the right people who will responsibly get the work done. Every time there is an issue or a task that has to get done, find the person within the team who is responsible of doing it and show him how to do it. This might take you more time than if you'd have done it yourself. However, if you do each task yourself, it robs you of the ability to focus on the big picture of the business.

You have to develop the mission and vision of the company. You should constantly make sure that you have the right team in place and that the right projects are being worked on. You can't be working 'in' the business and 'on' the business at the same time.

Even if you are a small business owner and at the moment think that you can't afford to hire all the team members that you need, you still want to look into all the different areas of your business – sales, marketing, operations and finance – and individualize projects in each one of them to focus on every week. For the time being, you will fulfill the roles of your missing team members, until you reach the point where you can afford to hire them. And when you do hire, you will know exactly who to hire and what their responsibilities will be.

There is a big difference between 'doing whatever it takes to keep the business going' and 'working on many projects simultaneously to get the business to the next level.' If you are doing whatever it takes you are probably busy but not focused. This usually means that you will stay busy forever. Why? Even if you decide to hire help, you will likely end up hiring yet another person who knows how to stay busy. You will delegate half of your busyness to him, and within a few weeks both of you will be busy full time again, and the cycle will repeat itself.

On the other hand, if you are focused on projects and you need help, you know exactly what you are looking for. You need someone to take over the responsibility of delivering the result needed, and sometimes you may find that outsourcing the project is the best choice for the business.

Hire For Attitude and Train For Skill

One of the most important lessons that I have learned over years of working with hundreds of employees in various positions is the importance of hiring for attitude and training for skill. You can train anyone for a skill. With time and passion, they will be able to perform skillfully. However, you can't change their attitude, and if they have a bad one, it will come back to haunt you no matter how skilled they are.

In the old economy, employers wanted academic degrees and solid experience when hiring. In today's new economy, that degree and that experience might not be worth much. In a world where everything changes so quickly, employers need people who are positive and open-minded and will keep learning and adjusting to new opportunities.

Much of what we learn in school can be useless by the time we actually get to use the information. Alternately, the computer and Internet allows just about anyone to learn a new skill at any time of the day or night. So, there you have it: You can teach the right employee the necessary skills but not the right attitude.

Attitude means that the person in training has a passion in the area that you are focusing them on. You want to ensure that, with training, they will be able to take responsibility and deliver the results you need. More importantly, you need to like their attitude. Engage them in conversation about life in general, and ask them how they would handle certain situations. Listen and see if you like the way they answer these questions; attitude is something that you either have or you don't, and I believe that you can see it at the first interview.

How to Pay for Employees

Every business owner has his own approach to paying employees: Basic salary, bonuses based on performance, raises, paid vacation days, etc. I don't think there is any right or wrong way as long as you are very clear with them at hiring on how things are done. They shouldn't meet any surprises while they are on the job.

From my point of view, a balanced approach is to pay a fixed salary with added profit sharing. This profit-sharing structure should be based on the results that they are responsible to deliver or their performance in communicating with customers and building the company's brand.

This approach gives you the confidence that everyone is as focused on the bottom line as you are, and it gives the employees the excitement of knowing that they can earn more money from their effort in growing the business.

But you have to make sure that this approach doesn't hurt the bottom line. For example, if you are giving people more money based on an increase in sales, make sure that their actions don't increase sales with a lower profit margin.

If they have the authority to change the sales price and sell it for less, you want to make sure to compensate them based on the markup of the product and not on the actual sale price, because you don't want them to keep selling at a lower markup just to get more sales going.

Some owners will go as far as giving all employees a percentage of the net profits of the company. Although this keeps everyone focused on the bottom line, most bosses are not comfortable with the fact that all employees will know how much profit the company makes.

Some business owners will take a percentage of the company profit and split it equally between all employees. This creates a team effort where all employees feel that all their actions affect both the bottom line and how much the team will earn at the end of the year.

Either way, you want to engage employees as much as you can with the bottom line of the company. They should feel that they are part of the success of the company and that they will benefit from it.

Show Appreciation

Salary is important – your employees have to pay bills and put food on the table. But for the productivity of the company and the long-term success of the team, it is equally important to show employees that you appreciate their work and respect them. More than anything else people want to feel appreciated and respected. As humans, we will all do a lot more in order to receive appreciation than to get more money. Feeling respected and appreciated is an innate need that we all have.

Some business owners fear that if they show their employees too much appreciation they will be taken advantage of and the employees will not do their jobs well. I think that if you balance appreciation and respect with being clear about your expectations (as well as monitoring that these are met), then you shouldn't have these problems. If you do feel that some employees are taking advantage of your appreciation, it may be because of their attitude, not because you are being nice to them.

Outsource or In-House

In recent years, the concept of outsourcing has become very popular. Today, there are companies outsourcing everything from sales to bookkeeping to order processing and more. The advantage of outsourcing is that you can find people who are really talented in one specific area and pay them only for the results they deliver. If you don't like their results, find another freelancer who might deliver better ones.

Outsourcing carries many advantages and most companies can likely find a few areas of their business that would make sense to outsource. Outsourcing keeps your overhead low since you are only paying for results. It's a lot easier to calculate your profit margin if you are only paying for results. Also, outsourcing means that you don't have to pay for sick days, vacation days, lunchtime, or any benefits or perks.

The advantages of having someone full time is that, if you have full time work in that particular area of your business, it might be cheaper to hire a person to do it in-house than to constantly outsource it.

Whether outsourcing or not, I would strongly advise you to look at your team members as if you outsource those areas of your business to them. Be very clear with them and with yourself as to which responsibilities you are delegating to them. Do they have a clear understanding of the outcome? How is their success measured?

POINTS TO REMEMBER!

- A successful enterprise consists of team members who are focused on results
- Give employees responsibilities that match their unique abilities
- Give employees the space to develop and grow
- Being busy and being efficient are not the same thing
- Hire for attitude and train for skill.

Chapter 8

YOUR ULTIMATE SALES TEAM

Everyone is Selling!

Everything begins with a sale. Most conversations that we have during the day are sales conversations, regardless of whether your official business title is 'sales person' or not. You are convincing customers to buy. You are persuading vendors to give you more buying credit. You are convincing an employee to take a lower pay raise. You are constantly selling your way of seeing things to those around you.

Selling is an amazing opportunity to help your customers fill a need with a product or a service that you provide. Today's world would be very different if not for people selling their ideas and for those people who took these ideas and made them into reality.

Columbus had to sell his Queen on his vision of new lands, or he wouldn't have discovered America. Every new invention starts with someone selling their idea to investors or to the marketplace. Without your ability to sell your idea, there is no chance for that idea to take off. The main driving force that keeps any economy going is the ability for its people to keep selling.

The Selling Mindset

The success of your ability to sell and conversely the lack thereof has a lot to do with your mindset and beliefs about selling. Years ago, researchers discovered that when we are in conversation, a full 53% of our communication happens through our body language and its energy vibrations as we communicate. Even if the conversation is on the phone, 38% is the tonality of voice and the way you speak, and only 9% of the communication comes through the actual words that we use.

What's amazing about this discovery is that you can say all the wrong words in your sales conversation and still have a 91% of getting the right message across and achieve your desired results. On the other hand, you can say all the right words, and still have a 91% chance of getting the wrong message across and not accomplish what you want.

This is why you really have to be passionate about what you do, because your real feelings will come across when you communicate. Your passion will help you achieve your vision in life and in business. Most entrepreneurs who are just starting out in business need to sell their vision to investors and vendors because they need help to get started. In most cases, the entrepreneurs who are successful in convincing others to help them with resources and money are those who are passionate about their vision and communicate their passion with a high vibration of positive energy. Others can't help but be pulled in since energy is contagious to everyone around it.

On the other hand, you will find some sales people who approach you without passion or positive energy being transmitted. Even if you already know about their product or service, and even when there is no need to convince you about it, you will likely find that you have no interest to engage in conversation with the sales person, because there is no passion.

We all have those moments when we walk away from a sales conversation after we bought the product or service, and we ask ourselves, "Why did I buy this?" We may not be able to explain why we did, but something happened during that sales conversation that made us feel good. That made us buy the product in order to keep the connection with the sales person who gave us that good feeling; having the product will keep reminding us of that experience.

This happens on a subconscious level – it's a natural process that we don't control. Check your gut while you're in the middle of a conversation: Are you enjoying it or is it making you feel stressed? The more relaxed and passionate we feel in a conversation, the greater the chances are that the other person feels the same way.

If you find that you don't enjoy having a sales conversation about your company, it is time to work on your underlying beliefs as we discussed in Chapter 3. It's not an easy process but definitely worth the effort. With every belief that you change you will see major changes in your results. You will also feel a lot more energized and excited about what you do.

Why Most Sales Training Doesn't Work

Most sales trainings focus on telling you how to sell, teaching you what to say and how to respond to objections. But we now know that what you say only accounts for 9% of your communication. Most sales training ignores the other critical part: not **what** you say, but **why** you say it, and how you **feel** about yourself and the product or service you are selling.

Every time you attempt to make a sale, look where your focus is. Is it on yourself needing to make the sale in order to achieve a sales target or make a commission,

> *"You can get anything you want in life if you help enough other people get what they want in life."*
>
> Zig Ziglar

or is it on your customer and how you can help him with his needs in order to improve his life and business?

Every product or service is designed to improve something in life or it wouldn't exist. You have the choice to focus on that need and how that can help your prospect.

One of the big differences between focusing on your needs vs. focusing on the customer's needs is that if all you care about is making a sale and getting commissions, it doesn't matter to you whether the prospect needs the product or service. It doesn't matter if you can fill a need for him and improve his life, because all you care about is that you make your sale. Your prospect will feel this in the communication and will resist your selling attempts by finding excuses to push you away and hope that you never come back to try again.

The sales conversation should be a discussion about whether what you have to offer is the right fit for what that prospect needs. You should then let the customer help you determine his need for your product or service.

We Hate To Be Sold To, But We Love To Buy

We all have a built-in antenna that goes off when someone tries to sell us something. We have all been burned in the past by agreeing to buy something and then regretting our decision when it was too late. We have created a built-in alarm system to defend us from falling into that trap again.

Unwanted sales approaches happen often. Consider those times, during dinner, when your home phone rings and the guy on the other end says, "Hello! This is John calling from XYZ Company. Do you have a minute to talk?" Most of us will put down the phone or say that we aren't interested. If I were to then ask you what that caller wanted and why you put down the phone you would say, "Telemarketer!" Now, what if that telemarketer had something to offer that you desperately need right now? Maybe he can save you a lot of money on you cell phone bill or on your energy bill. "Why wouldn't you listen to him?"

The answer is that regardless of what he has to offer, we have a preconceived belief that he does not have our best interest in mind. We are afraid that if we let him talk, we will be persuaded and make a bad decision that we will later regret. In order to avoid that trap, we will push away anything that looks like a sales attempt.

The only way we will buy is if we decide that we need something and we reach out to buy it. This makes us feel fully in control of the process. Alternately, if we get introduced to a sales person by a trusted friend who is confident in that sales person we may give him the opportunity to help us.

This may seem like a simple concept – and it is – but it makes all the difference in the world. This is the difference between success and failure in sales. Change your mindset. Look at what you do as an opportunity to help other people improve something in their life or business. Focus fully on your prospect's needs and you will find that people will be a lot more interested in listening to you.

Another benefit is that when you are really focused on the customer's needs, people will be confident in referring others to you. They will trust that you will only sell to their friends if it is in their best interest and that you will walk away if it is not – may it not be the right time for the prospect to buy, or may it be that a competitor's product or service would be a better fit for them.

Today's consumers are overwhelmed with a nonstop flow of information and sales pitches. It has become very difficult to get people's attention and have them focus on what you have to offer. Many people have turned to social media for their friends to help them decide what to buy. Most business today is done through word of mouth, and you want to be in a position where people feel comfortable referring you to others. People, in general, fear recommending a product or a service to friends. They always ask themselves, "What if that friend is upset that we pushed them into something that they didn't really need?" The only way people will refer you is if they are confident that you will always do the right thing with everyone.

Remember that this is not another sales technique. You can't fake sincerity; people can tell whether you are sincere or not. You really have to program your mind to be focused on your customers and their needs. And believe me, the money will follow.

How Many Sales Channels Do You Have?

Sales are the driving force in most businesses. If you have a constant flow of new sales, you can figure out how to manage the other parts of the business. If sales die down, though, there is nothing left to work with. This is what puts sales as the number one issue to first focus on in your business. Even if the underlying issue as to why the business is not succeeding is in another part of the business, as long as we can keep sales coming, we will have peace of mind to focus on any other parts without fear of ending up with a successful operation but no sales.

Of the most important questions in any business is how many sales channels you have. There are many different sales channels. In most cases, you should have more than just one that is generating sales for your business.

> *"The operation was successful but the patient died..."*
>
> Source unknown

Let's take a closer look at some of the sales channels that a business can have.

You can sell through in-house sales representatives, outside sales representatives, independent sales people, off-line marketing, online marketing, affiliates, and direct mail, call centers, etc. Each one of these channels has advantages and disadvantages. It's important that you keep looking at adding more sales channels to increase your sales leads and your business.

A great example is off-line vs. online marketing. Until a few years ago, most brick-and-mortar businesses didn't even explore the option of going online. They saw themselves as an offline business and didn't see the need for an online presence. Even today, I still find a whole lot of storeowners that haven't thought about having presence online. They still look at their business as being a local-based store. They don't realize that no matter what you do, there is always a way to use the web to increase your sales. Even if you can't sell directly online, you can use the online tools to increase awareness for your business.

For example, a local store can have a website that lists in-store specials, or offers customers the opportunity to reserve an item before they come in to the store. Many customers today prefer the web to the phone, and giving them the opportunity of communicating with your store via the web is a great tool to increase your brand and expand your loyal customer base.

We are using the web today as our phone book to find locations and phone number when we need them. The question is, will customers find your information when they need it? People from your neighborhood might be shopping online for products or services that you offer without realizing that you can help them. Will they find your company as a resource when they search?

A simple Google search will give you the answer.

Building a Great Sales Team

With the right sales team in place, you can take your business from a small startup to a large, successful enterprise in less than two years. All it takes is a clear plan and a lot of hard work.

The dream of most business owners is to have a well-oiled and motivated sales team who are on the road all day selling their product or service. Over the last ten years I have spent a lot of time hiring, training and coaching sales teams for my clients. This is something I am passionate about. From coaching a nationwide team of real estate agents to giving a 30-hour crash course in sales, here are a few lessons learned along the way:

Give Your Team a Clear Vision for their future.

Hiring and maintaining a successful sales team takes a lot of work. In order to be successful you need a plan. Good sales people like to join a company that has a clear plan for their success, for how they can reach their desired income and success.

They need to hear from you how they will be trained and what support they will get. They want to know about your most successful sales people. They want the confidence that they will be able to sell your product or service, and that they will be well compensated for doing so.

It might be difficult to create such a plan if you are just starting out, but if you invest the time to do so, it will be a lot easier for you to attract successful sales people to join your company.

You can't predict who will succeed.

Logically, we should be able to know who will succeed as sales representatives, based on talent and communication style. But, after years of trying to identify the characteristics of successful sales people, I have come to the conclusion that you can't predict who will succeed.

I have seen sales people who had all it takes to succeed and were confident that they would, but they couldn't get their first sales closed even with months of training and coaching.

On the other hand, some of the most successful sales people that I've worked with are people that I wouldn't hire (even after seeing their success) because they don't have the characteristics that we think a sales person should have. Some of these are stutterers, unsociable, etc., yet they are still top sales people in their industry and have had unbelievable success.

The common denominator I see among all successful sales people is persistence; they will keep going long after the unsuccessful sales people gave up.

Below are statistics that show the power of persistence. Sales trainers have used these metrics worldwide for many years.

Follow up statistics:

- 48% of salespeople never follow up with a prospect, after their initial contact
- 25% of salespeople make a second contact and then stop
- 12% of salespeople make three contacts with their prospects and then stop
- Only 10% of salespeople make more than three contact attempts with their prospects

Now let's look at closing statistics.

- 2% of sales are made on the first contact
- 3% of sales are made on the second contact
- 5% of sales are made on the third contact

- 10% of sales are made of the fourth contact
- 80% of sales are made on the fifty to the twelfth contact

This explains why 10% of salespeople close 80% of sales, while the other 90% of salespeople are only closing 20% of total sales made.

> *"Nothing in this world can take the place of persistence. Talent will not; nothing is more common than unsuccessful people with talent. Genius will not; unrewarded genius is almost a proverb. Education will not; the world is full of educated failures. Persistence and determination alone are omnipotent."*
>
> Calvin Coolidge

Care for them on a personal level.

Being in sales is challenging, you have to stay motivated and keep going even as you are constantly rejected. Sales is a constant struggle and it takes a lot of strength to stay balanced and focused on reaching your goals. If you build a strong relationship with your sales team and show them that you care for their success on a personal level and want them to succeed, it will give them a lot of courage to grow and succeed.

I find that some business owners have a hard time getting close to their sales people; they feel that it's not professional because it's all about business. Nothing could be further from the truth! Your ability to build a strong personal relationship with your sales team and employees could be your biggest contribution to building a strong company. It could also give you more satisfaction than the money the company earns you.

All your sales people have dreams and visions for their future. Your ability to listen and understand these goals and dreams and help your people achieve them will help them grow on a personal level. This, in turn, will lead to a success for your company as well.

All your sales people also have issues and problems in life, as we all do. If they feel they can discuss these things with you and that you care for their wellbeing and that of their family, they will grow and develop a lot faster to use their real talent and passion and create great results for your company.

Give them the best training you can.

The more they know about the product or service they are selling, the more successful they will be. Knowledge builds confidence to start conversations with prospects, because the sales person knows that they will have something valuable to share and discuss.

Give them sales training. Either by sharing and discussing your experience with selling your product or service, or by giving them access to professional sales training. Selling is an art that can be learned and constantly improved. Every time you hear a sales training or a motivational speech from an experienced sales person you will learn something new, expand your thinking and generate new ideas on how to build better business.

Hold them accountable.

Have weekly meetings with your sales team to discuss results, issues and opportunities, and to set clear goals for what they have to accomplish. Hold them accountable: good sales people want to grow fast and they gain motivation from setting goals and reaching them.

I find that the best way to set goals is to have the salesperson choose his own goals for the week or the month and then discuss how he will reach them, making sure that he has a plan of action for reaching these goals. People will do a lot more to reach a goal that they've set themselves, than a goal that was forced on them.

It doesn't matter how big or small the goal is. As long as they can tell you what actions will get them there and they can realistically see themselves reaching it, you should accept it, even if the goal is too small according to your expectations. If they practice the habits of goal setting and accountability, they will slowly increase their goals to meet your expectations.

You have to believe in it.

In order to succeed in any sales, you have to really believe in the company and the product or service that you are selling. You have to feel that the company will deliver a great product or service that's better than the competition. If a sales person questions your ability to deliver a great product or provide a great service, he or she will not be able to sell it because prospects will sense the lack of excitement and conviction in the company.

Ask your sales people if they feel confident in the company. If they do not, perhaps they are lacking information about the company, or perhaps you have some work to do to improve your operations. It's important to have a discussion about confidence level to make sure they are excited about the product or service and the solutions it offers to the marketplace.

Sales People Versus Strategic Relationships

Having full-time sales people that focus on your product or service has its advantages. They work all day long to bring in new sales, and their livelihood depends on their constantly bringing in new sales leads, which generate revenue for your company.

But not every business can afford this. It's time consuming to find the right people and it takes a lot of time and money to train them until they can bring in sales. This might not be an option for you at this point in time.

That said, you could always build strategic relationships, and so generate business without the downsides of full-time sales people. If you do this right, you can create a great sales channel that will provide constant sales leads for your business.

Start by looking out for anyone who already has a strong relationship with your ideal customer. Look for sales people who offer another product or provide a service to this ideal customer. Ask them if they would be interested in helping you get more sales by either referring business to you or selling for you. Offer them compensation that makes sense for both of you and give it a trial period to see if the situation works for both of you. If it works, you can use that as a model to find similar relationships in other fields or geographic areas.

If for whatever reason it didn't work out, try to learn from it to see what you can do differently with the next potential relationship. Immediately start building the next relationship, until you find a model that works for your business.

Your Customers As Your Sales Team

Your biggest potential sales teams are your customers. If you build a strong relationship with them, they will naturally send business your way. You can speed this process up by creating incentives for them.

A while ago, we created a marketing program for a client who runs a fashion store. Every customer who bought at his store was sent a "thank you" letter four weeks after visiting. The letter had two coupons inside, both for 12% off any purchase. One coupon was for the customer to use and one was for them to give to a friend. The letter encouraged them to bring a friend along. Within three months sales in this store had increased by 27% and 82% of all coupons mailed out were redeemed.

How can you involve your customers to help them sell your product or service?

POINTS TO REMEMBER!

- How you feel about yourself and your product, is more important than how you sell it
- We hate to be sold but we love to buy
- Hold your sales people accountable for delivering results
- Get your customer to sell for you

Chapter 9

MARKETING FOR THE NEW ECONOMY

The Definition of Marketing

Marketing is about relaying your message to the world. Every business has a message, but your potential customers might not know yours. Marketing sets the stage for you to communicate your message to the public; to tell them about your business and what it can do for them.

Conveying your message is great as long as you have something exciting to say or a unique edge to your business. It has to be a message that the marketplace is waiting to hear because it solves a need for them or it gives them a pleasure that they currently don't have.

However, if there is nothing that distinguishes your business from your competitor's, then that's what your message will communicate to the marketplace.

Imagine if I gather all of your potential customers in one big room and give you the opportunity to give a 30-second speech on the message of your company, what it can do for them, and why they should do business with you. What would you tell them?

I find that the message is weak with most businesses. It would say something like, "Look, we have a business! We sell this generic product. There is not much difference between us and our competitors, but we do have sales and specials occasionally." These businesses may just as well say, "Come and buy from us. We have a lot of bills to pay and we need your cash!"

Think about your favorite brand. Imagine their CEO getting up on stage and giving a 30-second speech about what their company can do for you. What would they say?

Your marketing can only be as good as your message. If you don't have a clear, strong message, you are spending your money to tell people that you don't have a strong reason for them to shop with you.

If you haven't figured out a clear message and a unique selling proposition of what your company stands for, go back to Chapter 5 and reread it!

How Marketing Has Changed Over The Years

Marketing has changed a lot over the last few years and it keeps on changing. New platforms are being created all the time, and these can help you get your message to more people than ever before. But this also creates more confusion than ever before in determining the right marketing plan for your business.

From 1960-2000, the average person watched television and read the newspaper to get his daily dose of information. In turn, most companies used these channels to market their product or service in the form of ads or commercials.

A television commercial or ad in a major newspaper would bring immediate results, and was part of every large company's marketing budget. Smaller companies who couldn't afford these channels used local newspapers or radio stations to get their message out to the masses. Starting by the late 1990's, this began to change as more and more people started using cell phones and the Internet. The way we communicate and get our information has changed forever. The average person today is exposed to over 30,000 messages each and every day. This volume makes it impossible to filter and organize data efficiently.

Even those who still read newspapers are not paying as much attention to the printed ads because we have programmed our brain to ignore data in order to avoid being overwhelmed. People may look at an ad and see its content but not focus on which brand is advertising. We know that whatever we need we can look up in a simple Google search or ask our friends about what they are using, so we may find no need for to focus on ads.

The first car advertisement, in 1898, said, "Dispense with a horse and save the expense, care and anxiety of keeping it, to run a motor carriage costs about ½ cent per mile.... It easily manages 3 to 20 miles per hour" Everyone paid close attention to this ad because it was such a major invention and would change the way people lived.

When Ford came out with the Model-T in 1908, his ad read, "Eleven to seven! A merchant who knows says that it costs him eleven cents per delivery by horses.... And seven by Ford Cars..." Families would sit around their dinner table and read every word in the ad, then discuss whether the car was really a possible replacement for their horse.

Fast-forward 100 years: Every magazine and newspaper has many car ads, all of which look similar. Even if people are interested in a new car, it's not ads that will get them excited about what they want. They base their choices for their next car on what their friends talk about and drive. Or they rely on the current buzz between their friends and co-workers on Facebook and Twitter.

Engaging Versus Marketing

In the past, as we discussed, most marketing to the customer was done by way of commercials or ads that told potential customers what a business had to offer. The hope was that enough people would take action from seeing and hearing these ads.

But our new social media environment finds people spending most of their time communicating online with friends and with various different groups. Reaching today's customer has to be done by engaging them and marketing **with** them rather than **to** them.

Television and radio commercials as well as email blasts still have their place in marketing, but you can get a lot more return on your investment by engaging and educating prospects than by simply marketing to them.

In this social media era, entire brands have been built on Facebook, and some brands have been ruined with a few YouTube videos.

Let's take a closer look into Facebook, the world's largest social network. Of more than 800 million users in 70 languages, more than 50% log in daily. The average user has 130 'friends.' More than 250 million photos are uploaded daily.

It's too early in the social media age to understand its full power, but we have already seen that political regimes can fall by the use of social media. The rise in Egypt was kick started and maintained on Twitter and Facebook. In July of 2009, elections were held in Iran. The masses had fought for their freedom to elect without government tampering. The Iranian government banned all media members from its cities to avoid them updating on the elections. But for the first time in history, the people of Iran had a choice: they could communicate and join forces using social media. Millions joined in protests across Iran, being updated on developments via Twitter and other social media platforms.

Twitter was scheduled to go down for a few hours that night for maintenance and upgrades, but according to CNN, they got a request from the US State Department to postpone the scheduled maintenance so that the people of Iran could keep up pressure on the Iranian government. Since the US has no embassy in Iran, it used Twitter as its main source for getting updates from the ground in Iran.

People have become fed up with official media and are turning to their close friends and role models for some sort of safe haven with 'real' information.

If you can get your existing customer base to be excited about your product or service – by treating them as special; by offering them a unique customer experience, etc. – these customers will talk about it online. With an average of 130 social friends, this customer reporting online can get you many leads. What's best is that these leads will come to your business ready to buy, and you haven't had to spend one dollar on marketing to them.

Sales and Marketing

Sales and marketing must go hand in hand since the goal of marketing is to generate sales and in order to generate sales you need marketing to communicate your message to potential customers.

I find that many companies do not know how to combine sales and marketing. Many have two separate departments in their company, with each one doing its own thing. I see sales teams on the road or on the phone desperately looking for new sales and wishing they had better marketing to help them reach out to new prospects. Meanwhile, I see marketing teams designing material without really understanding what it takes for the sales people to make a sale for the business.

Sales and marketing have to work in coordination with each other. Marketing has to be created based on what the sales people need in order to get a sale. The sales team knows what objections their prospects have and the marketing team needs to address those issues. This will build consumer confidence and trust in your company.

If you hire a marketing company to create marketing for you, have them talk to your sales team and to your customers so they understand the buying process and the challenges of your business. Otherwise, they won't be able to create the right marketing concepts for you.

Branding or Marketing?

It's important to distinguish between branding and marketing. Mix these two up and you won't achieve the results you are after.

Branding is anything that you do to create your unique selling proposition. This includes the physical appearance of your store or office, your logo and company colors, and the way your phones are answered and customers are greeted. These create and maintain your brand.

Branding is not measurable. You can't know how many new customers you have because your brand image has improved. Still, branding is something that you have to do. It is the foundation of every successful company, and you can't start your marketing until you have created a brand.

Marketing, on the other hand, is made up of specifically targeted campaigns that communicate your brand's message to clients and prospects. Marketing has to be measurable and every marketing campaign – from ad placements to large mailings to social media campaigns – needs to be measured. You need to know if your resulting profit exceeded your investment in the project.

I find that companies keep placing ads out of desperation to generate sales, but they don't measure their results. They don't assess if the marketing is actually bringing in more than the investment in it. Placing ads without a built-in tracking method that will give you the results is, by definition, branding and not marketing.

When Coco Cola puts up a big billboard advertising their product, they can't measure the results of that ad and how much new sales it generated. They have a big budget for branding and will keep spending it even if they can't measure results. But that's Coca Cola. Most small business can't afford to spend too much on branding, not unless they have a clear, long-term plan for what they are trying to accomplish with it and how it will pay off.

Do You Need a Marketing Budget?

Since most companies have to use marketing in order to keep generating new sales, how do you decide how much to invest in your marketing?

Since marketing has to be measurable, the simple answer is that you start with a small investment. Create a marketing project with clear goals: what are you trying to accomplish, whom are you targeting, and what action you want them to take. Add into your campaign a way to measure the results; this will tell you if this campaign makes financial sense. If the campaign does give you a profit, you have figured out a marketing model that works for you. In most cases you can repeat this and keep getting great results.

If it doesn't work, analyze the details of the campaign to see why, and based on that information, create a new campaign and test it to see if it generates profit.

Many companies create a marketing budget at the beginning of their year and keep spending until the allocated money runs out. They then wait until their next budget comes around.

From my point of view, this approach doesn't make sense. If you measure the results of your campaigns and find that they turned a profit for you why do you need a limit on your marketing spending? You can keep repeating your proven system over and over, generating more profit.

On the other hand, if you can't or you just don't measure the results of your marketing, why spend any money at all? You might be losing money on these campaigns, in which case your company will make more money if you just keep the marketing budget in your account without spending it.

In the old economy, all big companies had huge marketing budgets and spent millions each year without knowing if those campaigns were working! In the new economy you can't afford to do that; everything has to me measured for results.

Google AdWords is a good example of result-driven marketing. You can set up a campaign to attract traffic to your site by paying Google for every click that potential customers make on your ad that takes them to your site. A conversation code tells you how many orders you got from these clicks and how much money they spent on your site.

At the end of the day, you look at how much you spent on this campaign, what the click-through rate was and what profit it generated for your business. If you made money on the AdWords campaign, you can increase your daily spending budget and increase your traffic and rake in more profit. When something like this works out for you, you will discover that you have created a marketing channel that can keep feeding your business with a constant flow of new sales.

You can also repeat this process on Bing or any of other online PPC (pay-per-click) channels and increase the results drastically, knowing that you are not risking your money since you know that the formula works for you.

If you lost money on your campaign, try to change the keywords you used. Study your customers to understand which keywords they would use when they search for your product, or you can change the message in the ad and test to see if that would work better. Either way, you have a clear way of measuring whether your marketing is profitable or not.

In truth, that's the way every marketing campaign should be done. When I develop a marketing plan for clients, I put in a tracking system that will tell me the campaign's actual profit. Based on the results, we design the next campaign.

Everything in marketing has to be tested, since no one can really predict what the results will be like. I have seen certain ads outperform others by 200% without any logical reason. You might find that an ad placed in one newspaper or magazine will outperform other newspapers and magazines by a few thousand percent. Could be because more of your potential customers are reading that source, or maybe they just take those ads more seriously than the other sources.

I recently ran a national marketing campaign where we placed ads in 65 magazines and newspapers. Each ad had a coupon in it and a bar code that was unique to each publication. This made it very easy to run a report and see the actual sales and profit generated from each publication.

The results were fascinating as some publications outperformed others by serious numbers. In our report, we added our cost to place the ad in that publication, and created a column in excel that showed the percentage of profit or loss on each investment. Some of the publications didn't generate even one sale while others brought in huge profits.

The first week report showed:
- *The total cost of the investment was $29,250*
- *The campaign's net profit was $16,000*
- *The profit margin was 54%*

The second week, we only put the ad in those publications that generated a profit.

The second week report showed:
- *The total cost was $11,700*
- *The gross profit was $23,800*
- *The net profit was $12,100*
- *The profit margin was over 100%*

Since we didn't lose money on any of the unprofitable publications, we put in less and took out way more.

The Lifetime Value of a Customer

One of the important concepts in marketing is the lifetime value (LTV) each customer holds for your company. In most cases, a customer is not a one-time customer. Rather than making a one-time purchase, a customer gives you more business in the future. This future business may include them signing up for monthly membership or placing orders every time they need your product or service.

You can figure out your LTV by running reports on how long the average customer stays with your company and how much they spend with you over that period. If your average customer stays with you for three years and spends $10,000 at a net profit of 20% for you, your LTV per customer is $2,000.

This number can help when you do a marketing campaign since it lets you look at it from the perspective of how much you can afford to spend to acquire a new customer. If a mailing campaign costs you $10,000 and you get 10 new customers from it, the LTV of those 10 new customers is $20,000 over the next three years, which means that your return on investment on the campaign is 100%.

If you only look at the first purchase the newly acquired customer will make, the profit will be a lot less than if you look at their LTV. Keep in mind, though, that you can only look at the LTV if you are confident that you have the system in place to take care of your customers and turn their first visit into a long-term relationship with your company.

Getting Social

One of the biggest changes in the last few years is the rise and explosion of social media networks, from Facebook to Twitter to Google Plus and countless others, new opportunities have been created, and the way we communicate has drastically changed.

Just to get an idea on how powerful those platforms are, let's look at a recent report that shows what happens now online every 60 seconds:

- 100 new accounts are opened on LinkedIn
- 320 new accounts are opened on Twitter
- 6,600 pictures are uploaded to Flicker
- 13,000 iPhone applications are downloaded
- 600 new videos are upload to YouTube
- 168 million emails are sent
- 695,000 Facebook statuses are updated
- 510,040 Facebook comments are posted

All that happens each minute of each day.

People are communicating through these social media channels about every topic on earth. This creates opportunities for you. Become part of these communications, and you can build a loyal following of customers that will buy from you and refer their circles of influence to you.

Research shows that 81% of small businesses in the US have attempted, over the last 12 months, to create an online presence, but only 16% are generating business online.

Let me share some points that I found very helpful in building an online presence.

PICK A PLATFORM AND COMMIT TO IT FOR ONE FULL YEAR

It takes time to build a following on any social network. It takes time for people to trust you and recommend their friends to check your platforms. If you keep moving from one social network to the next, you will never build up a strong presence in any one of them.

Do some research to determine which platforms will best service your needs based on your industry. Pick one or two that seem the most promising, and commit to a full year of activity to build a strong following there.

PROMOTE YOUR SOCIAL EXISTENCE

Link to your social page anywhere you can. Add the link to your outgoing email signature, and use it on all your company marketing materials. People who know about you but are not ready to buy from you yet will connect with you. This will allow them to learn more about you and get comfortable purchasing from you at a later time.

COMMUNICATE AS A PERSON, NOT A COMPANY

People like to connect to people rather than to companies. Communicate as you would on your personal social page but with company and industry information. Trying to make all postings formal and corporate will bore people and they will stop following you.

IT'S NOT ABOUT YOU

Put yourself in the customers' position; think what type of information they would be interested in reading or watching online. It's fine to post news about a new product or a sale you're having, but if you want people to continue following you long-term, you have to give them interesting, helpful and useful information.

DON'T OVER-POST

Two or three posts per day are more than enough. If you post too much, people will stop reading, because we are limited to how much time we can spend on reading other people's posts, even if we like the brand. If you post too much, people will push off reading them for a later time when they think they will have more time. And that almost never happens.

Also, never post the same announcement more than once. Doing this will train your followers to ignore your posts since they have learned that it isn't all new content.

ENGAGE THEM AS MUCH AS POSSIBLE

Create contests where people can win things if they answer a question or leave feedback on your product or services. Any opportunity to engage readers and gather responses will increase loyalty and will bring new followers.

The Right Marketing Plan

Every business is different, and your marketing plan should be uniquely designed to meet your business' needs. Let me share some general points that apply to most marketing plans.

CREATE MULTIPLE CHANNELS

Take out a blank piece of paper. Write your company name in the middle of the page and draw a box around it. Draw four lines from the box corners to the 4 edges of the page. On each line write down one marketing channel that you are currently using. For example, your four channels could be, 1-placing ads in newspapers, 2-pay-per-click (PPC), 3-search engine optimization (SEO), and 4-direct mail.

If you don't yet have four different marketing channels, then try to think of new ones. Think of other industries and how they market their product or service. Can you adapt any of those channels for your business? If you do have four marketing channels now, analyze whether they are working well for you. If they aren't, consider which new channels you can add to replace the ones that are not working.

HAVE A CLEAR OUTCOME FOR EACH CHANNEL

This is very important. What do you want people to do after they see or hear your marketing? Do you want them to know about a special sale? Do you want them to generally know what you offer? Do you want them to contact you? Knowing such details before you start will make it a lot easier to design the project and meet those needs.

KEEP IT SIMPLE AND INFINITELY CLEAR

The best marketing campaigns and ads are those with a lot of empty space. The fewer words and the simpler the campaign, the more people will pay attention and take action.

Most ads I see are so packed with information that it's hard for the brain to summarize what's going on. Some businesses think that because they are paying for an ad, they have to make sure to use up every inch on the page. People are exposed to so much information today that they have learned to ignore anything that looks complicated.

I recently saw a sign in a public bathroom. The sign said, "For more information on lung cancer, keep on smoking!" No pictures, no long speeches, no statistics – just 9 words in big letters on a white background. The message was so clear and powerful that I kept on thinking about it for a long time. This, I believe, is brilliant marketing, and all advertisements should have the same affect if they are done right.

POINTS TO REMEMBER!

- Your marketing can only be as good as the uniqueness of your business
- Marketing has to be measured
- You don't need a marketing budget, you need clear reporting on the ROI for each marketing project
- Engage with your customers on their social platforms

Chapter 10

PUTTING IT ALL TOGETHER

As you've read through the chapters of this book, you were offered many new beliefs and perspectives in how to look at business and life. This is not a step-by-step guide per se. Since we all are unique in our own way and have to create our own vision and mission for life and business, there is no one-size-fits-all approach. This book, however, has given you some food for thought and some excellent new tools that you can utilize in creating your own story and leave your unique footprint behind.

Let me share with you some final thoughts that might be helpful on your journey.

Time Management Is a Waste of Time!

You are constantly struggling to manage your time better. Every morning you start your day determined to use your time efficiently and focus on the important things. Yet, ten hours later, you are looking at your desk and all the important things are still sitting there waiting patiently to be taken care of. Another day has passed, and you still haven't figured out how to manage your time better.

"There has to be an expert who will teach me how to manage my time better", you may think. "Surely, there are a lot of people who have figured out how to do this. Maybe I can sign up for a class, and learn their time management secrets once and for all."

The class is amazing and is loaded with so many good tips. You wonder why you didn't take this class years ago, as you could have saved so much time and have accomplished so much more! But it's never too late, and now you finally have a step-by-step process for organizing everything, for staying focused and for keeping your time managed. You plan on reviewing your seven pages of notes and to start managing your time first thing tomorrow morning – as soon as you get to the office.

Spring ahead several months. As you desperately search for an important document that's buried in one of the big piles on your desk, something suddenly occurs to you. Right there, in front of your eyes, are those seven pages of notes and a detailed time-management plan that you never implemented. You realize that the only thing they forgot to teach in class was where to find the time to implement the time-management plan!

You Can't Manage Time!

You can't manage your time; you can only manage your priorities. You are always making spur-of-the-moment decisions as to what the most important thing do right now is, and you somehow manage to find the time for it. You push everything else away, even using the excuse that you didn't have time for all the other things. Yet a better, truer answer would be that you didn't feel the importance of the other things enough to find the time to deal with them.

If you are working on the weekend to catch up on work and your child asks you to play a game with him, you might answer that you don't have time to play. But if, ten minutes later, that same child falls down and will need stitches, you **will** find the time to take him to the hospital and stay with him for as long as it takes.

When he got hurt, he became the most important thing on your to-do list. When he wanted you to play with him, your real answer was, "Spending time with you is not as important as me catching up on work." Of course, you'd never say that. You may even feel guilty that this thought passed through your mind. So you are covering it up with the excuse that you are busy.

The reason we are struggling with time management issues is because we are not exactly sure where we are going and what we have to do to get there. If we have a clear vision of where we are going and are committed to do whatever it takes to get there, we will do all things necessary.

I Am Busy

In the past, when most people worked in manufacturing, being busy was a sign of being successful. Being busy meant that you had orders to fill and if you had orders you had profits and were deemed successful.

In today's economy, being busy and being successful are not related. It might make you feel good that you are busy, but you can be busy all day long and end up losing money, while others can work for an hour or two a day and make a lot of money.

In the past, most people who had money were very busy running large factories or farms that employed many people and produced a lot of goods. In today's economy, successful people are those who find ways to create the most value in the marketplace with the least amount of time and overhead.

Being busy is an addiction that many people have, because it takes us away from the reality of life. If we are busy, we believe that we don't have to figure out what going on with us because we don't have time to think. Part of our brain may be telling us that something is wrong and that we should slow down and think about where we are going. Another part of our brain tells us to shut up and keep working. "You are busy and have a lot of things to do. There is no time for thinking and planning... Just get back to work."

I urge you to try the following experiment. Turn your phone off and find an empty table with nothing on it. Sit down, put your hands on the table and just breathe. You can think about anything

> *"It amazes me that most people spend more time planning next summer's vacation than they do planning the rest of their lives."*
>
> Patricia Fripp

you like but you can't do anything. You just have to sit there and think.

If you are like most people, you will get nervous after about one minute and start looking for something to do. That's because unless we have a clear vision and plan of where we are going and what we have to do, we will feel lost. Feeling lost is frightening to humans, since our highest need is to feel safe and secure. To avoid feeling lost, we keep busy pretending that we know what we are doing, and even if we don't know, it's still not a problem because we are BUSY!

This is the reason why most office desks are piled up from all sides with unfinished projects even though everyone agrees that you will be a lot more productive if you clean your desk and work on one thing at a time. But to work with a clean desk you really have to know what the most important task to focus on right now, because there is nothing else on the table... Since most people do not have a clear vision on what they are doing, they have a full desk with a lot of things that they are in the middle of, in order not to feel lost or insecure. There are a lot of things going on, regardless if those things are important and will get you to the next level, or make you money, etc.

The "busy addiction" also holds true for the use of social networks and cell phone texting. While there might be some benefits to communicat-

> *"The very worst use of your time is when you're doing something very well that doesn't need to be done at all."*
>
> Brian Tracy

ing on those networks, most people are addicted to them and waste hours communicating useless information that does not help them grow in any way. The networks do, however, help us feel busy: even in the 20-second wait for a traffic light to turn from red to green, we don't have to think. You can just take out your little toy and see the latest joke or status update on what your friend's friend will have for lunch today.

Remember: Keeping yourself busy is a temporary distraction from the reality that you need a clear plan of what you are doing and where you are headed.

Self Discipline

Success comes down to giving up what appears to be short-term comfort in order to gain long-term success. Every minute of every day we have a choice of how we are going to spend our time. We can do the things that are important to achieve our long-term success, or we can distract ourselves by doing things that feel momentarily satisfying.

Procrastination is a habit that we get into by not doing what we need to do in a timely manner. This creates a constant piling-up of things that became more and more urgent until we don't have a choice but to act upon the urgency in order to avoid trouble.

And after a while of this kind of behavior we convince ourselves that we actually don't have a choice since we have so many urgent things to take care of. And thus the cycle continues.

I was once attending a class by Richard Bandler, founder of NLP. After the lunch break, some people came back late. So he asked them, "How come that people who procrastinate, never procrastinate to procrastinate?" If those people have a habit of pushing everything off to a later time, why don't they push off being late to a later time, which would mean that they would for now **be** on time? The answer to this question is that people who procrastinate work hard to make sure they are always late, but they are not aware of the fact that they are doing it, since it is a habit.

Managing Priorities

In order to successfully manage our lives we have to create and organize our priorities and then make sure that we do the tasks necessary to archive our vision.

We discussed the concept of creating a vision in Chapter 2. Let's take that to the next step and create a vision that will be the guiding light for the focus of your energy and time.

FROM GOALS TO TASKS

Once you have a clear vision and a plan of how to get to your vision, it's time to create monthly goals that will help you make constant progress thwarts your vision.

Take your monthly goals and create a list of eight tasks that you will do this week in order to achieve your monthly goals. These eight tasks become your main focus for the week. Every day will start with this list: do as many as you can before you get busy and distracted with other things.

BE SPECIFIC

A task has to be very specific, or your mind will get lost on it. For example, making more money is not a specific or detailed task. It is too general, and your brain will get lost looking for ways to accomplish this task.

If one of your tasks for the week is to make more money, sit down at the beginning of the week and plan out what you are going to do this week specifically to make more money. Then, get that down to a detailed specific task, e.g. calling up ten potential new customers.

BE CONSISTENT

The key to success is consistency, because the more you do something, the more momentum you build and the easier it gets. There will be times when you will have an urge to skip a day or a week. Being persistent at those junctions will help you grow and will build you up to become the person who succeeds.

From my experience, the only way to manage your time is to start your week with a clear list of three to eight outcomes that you will accomplish during the week. Turn these into specific tasks that you can then start every day with and focus on until you get them done.

Coaching

Some people find that having a weekly coaching session helps them set their outcomes and tasks for the week. The biggest benefit of having a weekly coaching session is the accountability. There is another person that you know will ask you every week to report on your accomplishments.

Coaching also helps you get an outside view of your beliefs and limitations. We tend to get stuck by convincing ourselves of reasons why we can't do certain tasks even if we know they are important. A coach can help you find your limiting beliefs and work with you to change them into new and empowering ones.

Enjoy the Ride

Life is a journey that can be challenging. Some people wait for the challenges to stop and for things to settle down so that they can then begin living life. The problem is that by the time the challenges finish, life is practically over, and they've missed the whole point of life, which is to except its challenges and grow from them.

To sail through life we need a mixture of certainty and uncertainty. We like to be certain that the future will be good, but we also like the uncertainty and the sur-

> *"Happiness is like a butterfly: the more you chase it, the more it will elude you, but if you turn your attention to other things, it will come and sit softly on your shoulder."*
>
> Henry David Thoreau

prises that arise along the way. Without challenges, life has no meaning. The right mix of certainty and surprise means that you are sure you can handle everything that God sends your way. He has given you the tools and skills you need to deal with challenges and grow from them and develop into the real you.

Live in the Present – Trust the Future

I find that most of us live in the future. We think and worry so much about the future that we miss out on the present. Worrying about the future does not help us achieve a better future, it only keeps our focus on worrying instead of taking the necessary actions to create the future we want.

One of the old Jewish sages said that worrying is never appropriate, because you can either do something about your concern or you can't. So, if you can do something about your worry, do it, and why worry? If you can't do anything about it, why worry anyway?

Worry is a place in which we got comfortable at some point. Sometimes we stay in our worry bubble, thinking that we are doing ourselves some good by being responsible for our future.

But the reality is that worry does not help us in any way. It just keeps our focus on the negative possibilities of what could happen in the future. By focusing on that negativity, there is a good chance that some of our fears will actually come true. Whatever we focus on, we attract into our lives.

You want to plan for the future by creating your vision and by then working on achieve it by doing the daily tasks that will help you succeed.

> *"I have been through some terrible things in my life, some of which actually happened."*
>
> Mark Twain

Appreciate and Succeed

Take some time every day to appreciate all the good things in your life and be thankful to God for giving them to you. Start by appreciating the big things, like your family and health, and work your way to the smaller things like your cup of morning coffee. You can be grateful for everything. The more you appreciate, the more you will get. This has been proven by thousands of people over the years.

This is also a great tool for success in your social and business life since we all want to be around people who are happy and appreciative. None of us like to be around people who complain and always find the things that are not working out. Such people only keep focusing on the negative aspects of life.

Every day, thousands of things in our lives are working very well indeed. There are also things that are not working out the way we want. It's our choice where we place our focus.

The brain works like a camera: you can zoom in on anything and that will be what you will see and experience. It's like being at an event where you

> "The pessimist sees difficulty in every opportunity; the optimist sees the opportunity in every difficulty."
>
> Winston Churchill

can focus your camera to any part of the event. If you zoom in and capture a picture of people dancing, your impression of the event will be that people were happy and were having fun. On the other hand, if you zoom in on 2 people arguing with each other, your picture of the event will be that it was tense and noisy. The very same event can be seen from two different perspectives depending on what you zoomed in on.

Be Nice

Every person you meet poses as an opportunity for you to help his or her journey out. Be nice and offer compliments freely. Gestures like these will make people feel good and, in turn, will help you grow.

We all need the help of others to achieve our vision in life. The universe is one big puzzle where everyone helps everyone else in some way. Being nice to the people around you will help them grow more confident in pursuing their visions. In turn, they will be nice to their friends and family. Your little act of niceness can have a ripple effect beyond what you can imagine.

Always Do the Right Thing

We constantly have a choice about what do to and, for the most part, we know what the right thing is. This might not be the easiest thing to do or the most socially accepted thing to do, but it still is the **right** thing to do.

Always doing the right thing gives you peace of mind because you made the right choice and you don't have to be afraid of the results. This is true in life and in business. Sometimes, in the short term, it might seem like people who choose to do the wrong thing are rewarded. But in the long run they will always lose. Doing the right thing is the right thing to do. Always.

You can do it. Will you?

POINTS TO REMEMBER!

- You can't manage time – only priorities
- You can't speed up your way to success by being stressed about it
- Learn from the past – live in the present – trust the future
- Appreciate what you have and you will have more to appreciate
- Be nice to everyone, including yourself
- The right thing to do is to always do the right thing

To schedule a consulting session or for any other inquiries, you can contact me at **Askmaurice.com**

Made in the USA
Coppell, TX
27 August 2022

82184199R00111